MACKINTOSH & HIS CONTEMPORARIES

in Europe and America

General Editor
PATRICK NUTTGENS

JOHN MURRAY

Produced by Cameron Books, 2a Roman Way, London N7 8XG
Published by John Murray (Publishers) Ltd,
50 Albemarle Street, London W1X 4BD

Printed and bound by Richard Clay Ltd, Chichester, Sussex

First published 1988

Printed and bound in England

Designed by Ian Cameron
Edited by Ian Cameron and Jill Hollis

British Library Cataloguing in Publication Data

Mackintosh and his contemporaries:
  in Europe and America.
  1. Architecture, Edwardian
  I. Nuttgens, Patrick
  724.9'1   NA680

  ISBN 0-7195-4432-7

ACKNOWLEDGEMENTS
The conference upon which this book is based, held in Glasgow in August
1983 with the title *Charles Rennie Mackintosh: National and International*, was
the major event in the tenth anniversary celebrations of the Charles Rennie
Mackintosh Society.

  Acknowledgement is therefore made to the Society, to the steering committee
for the conference and in particular to Patricia Douglas, Director of the Society,
who was responsible for the organisation and management of the conference.
Special thanks are also due to Dr Frank Walker of the University of Strathclyde
for major and untiring help in the preparation of the manuscript and to Ann
Fairburn for typing and transcription.

  Filippo Alison acknowledges contributions to his paper by the translator,
Dr Bruno del Priore.

  Robin Lorimer acknowledges the help of Corinne Menage of the French
Institute in Glasgow in checking his translation of the paper by Claude Frontisi.

Frontispiece: Charles Sumner
Greene House, Pasadena,
California, 1901/1906/
1912/1914, by Greene and
Greene. Side elevation.
Beginning in 1901 as a one-
storey residence, Charles
Greene's own home ultimately
grew to three levels, and, with
each step of its growth and
evolution, its interiors were used
to explore new concepts and
details that later appeared in the
work for clients. The house is a
virtual textbook in the evolution
and refinement of the Greenes'
unique architectural vocabulary.

Footnotes have normally been positioned beside the relevant point in the text.
Where the quantity or length of the footnotes has made this impossible, they
have been numbered.

CONTENTS

INTRODUCTION

Roger Billcliffe

Charles Rennie Mackintosh's work and ideas were perhaps more widely disseminated than those of any architect before him, both through the medium of the specialist journals and magazines and by his personal visits to the centres of artistic unheaval in Europe. Through both these routes, Mackintosh seemed to act as a catalyst for his European contemporaries who were equally dissatisfied with the state of architecture and design in their various countries.

The title, 'Charles Rennie Mackintosh: National and International', chosen for the tenth anniversary conference of the Charles Rennie Mackintosh Society, at which the papers published in this book were given, was intended to reflect Mackintosh's international status. 'National', however, did not refer to his reputation in Scotland (which was negligible) but to his attempt to develop a modern style of building that reflected the national characteristics of Scottish architecture. Elsewhere in Europe, and in the United States, there was a similar revival of interest in the countries' traditional – vernacular – styles. Like Mackintosh, a number of young architects were looking beyond the 'international' styles of Gothic and Classical architecture towards the traditional forms employed by masons and builders in the many small houses and buildings which had not attracted the attention of wealthy patrons and their architects.

Was there, we asked ourselves, another 'international style', pre-dating that of the Bauhaus, which united Mackintosh's generation into one coherent movement? Did Mackintosh, Frank Lloyd Wright, Antoni Gaudí, Victor Horta, Hector Guimard, Josef Hoffmann and Edgar Wood share anything more than a common interest in the roots of architecture in their own countries? Were the new vernacular styles that they developed the result of Mackintosh's personal example, or did they all share the same sources of inspiration in the pioneering work of William Morris, Philip Webb, E.W. Godwin and others of their generation who had advocated a return to basic principles of form and function in design and architecture? Could the *Zeitgeist* be held responsible for this co-incidental outbreak of ideas sharing the same form or was the rapid spread of Mackintosh's idiom accounted for by new technology which allowed the almost simultaneous publication of illustrated articles across Europe?

The answers to some of these questions are immediately obvious. Gaudí's Moorish influences are very different from the Baronial sources of Mackintosh's Windyhill; Wright's Prairie Houses do not share kinship with the Glasgow School of Art. So any international style that can be identified in Mackintosh's generation has to be one of approach rather than one of vocabulary and form like the International Style that followed in the 1920s. Mackintosh's study of the past is well documented, his sketchbooks survive, and they are full of his immaculate drawings documenting almshouses, village halls, old monastic buildings and the organic growth of villages like Lyme Regis, Abbotsbury, Broadway and Chipping Campden. Was he alone in this first-hand study of the past? Had other architects in Austria or Germany made parallel studies before their first meeting with Mackintosh? Do their buildings display the same kind of historical eclecticism as his?

Although Mackintosh's methods had been studied in some detail, there was, surprisingly, very little published evidence of the practice of other architects and designers contemporary with him. Pevsner and more recent writers had laid the foundations for our knowledge of the situation in Britain. Here we could trace the development of the theories that made it easier for Mackintosh to make so dramatic a break from the accepted styles of his time. Had other architects in other countries followed a similar path, or was it Mackintosh's arrival within their midst, literally or metaphorically, which, particularly in Austria, Germany and Hungary, precipitated their move towards the new style? Certainly, Mackintosh was not likely to have advocated that they follow his stylistic vocabulary. He was, after all, designing for the Scottish climate and Scottish clients and, most importantly, he was working in Scotland. To follow his example, architects should search out the national characteristics of their own countries' architecture. It would have been dictated by the vagaries of the local climate, by the tastes of the local population and, above all, by the locally available materials and building techniques. That architects throughout the western world did this in the twenty years before the outbreak of World War I, is without doubt. Whether they did so with Mackintosh's encouragement was what the conference set out to discover.

Two other aspects of Mackintosh's career and personality formed other themes for the conference. The first, only lightly touched upon, was whether Mackintosh was, as Pevsner classified him, a pioneer of modern architecture (by which Pevsner meant the International Style) or whether he was simply a designer of integrity whose work remains relevant to architects in the second half of the twentieth century who have spurned the International Style for something they find more valid. The second question related to Mackintosh's role as a designer (of anything from furniture to cutlery), a field where many of the principles he applied to his buildings seem to have been set aside in favour of pure visual delight. This is an area where Mackintosh's influence both in Europe and America is more immediately obvious. His stylistic vocabulary can be found in designs from as far apart as Vienna and California. Was this the result of other designers listening to his theories on the role of the artist-architect working as designer, or was it purely the result of the visual inspiration of his work? In Vienna we know that it could have been, and was, both. But what of Gustav Stickley and the Greene brothers? Did they see Mackintosh through the pages of *The Studio* and *Dekorative Kunst* or are the similarities between their work and Mackintosh's purely coincidental?

By posing some of these questions and perhaps even answering a few of them, we hoped to resolve some of the imbalance in our knowledge about Mackintosh and his influence abroad. Was he unique, working in a vacuum, or was he at the forefront of a new wave of consciousness about the quality of design which swept the western world at the end of the nineteenth century? Did he inspire radical new thinking beyond his own shores, even though he had precious little effect on events in Scotland? Was he, as the Scots say (perhaps with a sense of self-denigration), a prophet without honour in his own land? If so, where did his honour lie and how was it achieved? A daunting list of questions to place before any set of conference-goers, but one, I think, which received a thorough response.

MACKINTOSH AND MUTHESIUS

Dennis Sharp

[1]Robert Kerr, *The Gentleman's House or How to Plan English Residences from the parsonage unto the Palace . . .* , John Murray, second edition, revised, London, 1865. *See* preface to the first edition, page *v*, W.R Lethaby referred to Kerr as 'a forgotten critic of ability'.

[2]Hermann Muthesius, *Das englische Haus*, was reissued in a second three-volume edition, again by Wasmuth of Berlin in 1908-11 with a new cover design, possibly by Frances MacNair. The same basic design was incorporated into the cover and title page of the first English edition edited, in one volume, by the present author as Hermann Muthesius, *The English House*, Crosby Lockwood Staples, London, 1979 (paperback: Blackwell, Oxford, 1987). Most of the quotations used in this paper are taken from Janet Seligman's translation, and the page references given here are to this edition. Both Hermann and Anna Muthesius became close friends of the Glasgow Four who all later visited the Muthesius's home in Berlin. Frances MacNair designed the cover of Frau Muthesius's book on national dress.

[3]Muthesius pp.9-10. But *see also* p.37.

[4]In a letter to the writer, January 1979.

In his original and provocative book, *The Gentleman's House* (1861), the Scottish-born architect and critic Robert Kerr wrote in an enthusiastic vein: 'It may be thought somewhat remarkable that the subject should not have been already exhausted, for it is well known that there are few *good* things so *good* – and therefore so well worth describing – as a *good* English house.'[1]

I shall come back to Robert Kerr later on, however unfortunate his choice of English might have been in the early 1860s! In fact, he polished it up in his brilliant examinations of house building plans and types in *The Builder* and elsewhere.

My subject is the English house and the many changes it underwent between the 1860s and the beginning of World War I – an arbitrary limit, perhaps, as the origins of the new movement in English domestic architecture can clearly be traced back to the 1840s, and the repercussions of this phase can also be seen continuing during the inter-war years in the furtherance of the new style of architecture of the 1920s. For our purposes it was in the 1860s that a domestic revolution began in middle-class housing as it sought to divest itself of the architectural styles advocated by architects used to working for the aristocracy.

'The end of the 19th century,' wrote Hermann Muthesius in his monumental three-volume work *Das englische Haus* (published by Wasmuth in Berlin, 1904–1905), 'saw the remarkable spectacle of a new departure in the tectonic arts that had originated in England and spread across the whole field of our European cultures.'[2]

This new departure began in the architecture of private houses. These buildings, Muthesius said, 'possessed everything that had been sought and desired: simplicity of feeling, structural suitability, natural forms instead of adaptations from the architecture of the past, rational and practical design, agreeably shaped rooms, the use of colour and the harmonious effect that had in former times resulted spontaneously from an organic development based on local conditions.' Muthesius was convinced that the English private house represented 'in every way a higher form of life.' 'The genuinely and decisively valuable feature of the English house,' he wrote, 'is its absolute practicality.'[3]

At the turn of the century, German interest in English cultural achievements reached a peak. It had probably originated with Queen Victoria's daughter, the Crown Princess Victoria of Germany, who had been responsible for introducing special bathrooms into the Palace in Berlin. Of particular interest to the Prussian court were aspects of British *Wohnkultur*, technical and industrial developments and fashion, as well as the aesthetics and writings of Thomas Carlyle, William Morris and John Ruskin (Hermann Muthesius devoted a whole magazine article to a discussion of Ruskin). *The Studio* magazine was widely read, and some new German art journals copied its style and format. According to R. Friedenthal, even the Emperor Wilhelm II – who was not noted for progressive views in matters of taste or choice of architects – was not unaffected by this English trend. Indeed, he goes on, 'Muthesius was one of the few modern architects who enjoyed his favour to some degree.' Friedenthal continued: 'It should not be overlooked that at the beginning of the century there was even politically an – unfortunately not lasting – movement of closer relations to Great Britain.'[4] Muthesius's own interest in English things continued up to the time of his death, although his later architectural work was by

*For a brief summary of this later work *see* Dennis Sharp, *Hermann Muthesius 1861-1927*, Architectural Association, London, 1979, and the comprehensive German language catalogue issued at the time of the Berlin exhibition, edited by Julius Posener and Sonja Günther and published by the Akademie der Künste, 1978.

no means as overtly influenced by his anglophile attitudes as his earlier villas set in their 'garden estates'.★

These views have been disseminated through many people's writings and are extremely well known. They help to illuminate a period of history but also, in a sense, wallpaper over it. No mere definition can possibly do justice to a period as important and truly wonderful as this late Victorian watershed. It saw revolution in most areas of human endeavour and most particularly in the creative and innovative arts and in the sciences. But it saw contentment in none. It was thoroughly agitated in mind and in body – in thought and gesture. In areas from biblical exegesis to ballet design, against a backcloth of great upheavals in society, writers and creative artists – including many architects, sought a new vision – a new way for the 'modern' world. My dilemma here is, in a sense, a traditional one – that of explaining the architectural aspirations of this period when a description that records architecture's phenomenal growth and charts its design changes reveals very little. Architecture is not autonomous, least of all the architecture of a country that was at the centre of the world arena. In order to be able to understand the architecture of the period, and in particular the domestic architecture, one must see it in the context of satisfying the romantic utopian and rural ideals that were shared (at times)

Hermann Muthesius (1861–1927).

Cover design by Frances MacNair for Anna Muthesius's book *Das Eigenkleid*, Berlin, ?1908.

with architects and artists from other countries – they constantly overlapped.

I shall start by examining the context of the English house in relation to an attitude of mind that prevailed in the second half of the nineteenth century: the 'modern' one. In looking for continuities as well as breaks within the prevailing traditions and trends between 1860 and 1914, I hope to place emphasis on the design ideas behind the housing developments of the decades around the turn of the century – that *fin de siècle* period which has been referred to by Holbrook Jackson as the 'banquet years'. When one examines such a period from a purely British viewpoint, it is only too easy to forget that in the United States an equally powerful revolution had been going on, culminating in the work of architects such as Frank Lloyd Wright. In France, too, in the optimistic ethos of the prevailing 'modernism', many utopian projects had emerged. The terms 'modern' and 'modernism', indeed, will recur many times. But 'modern' as a theme provides me with a cultural tin-opener to a period that has come increasingly under the microscopic examination of contemporary critics and historians.

The 'modern' attitude itself goes back to the middle years of the nineteenth century. More recently it has been seen as a term essentially applicable to the work of the twentieth-century artistic avant-garde. Clearly, it was equally relevant to the last decades of the nineteenth century. No other term is really applicable to a period that was transformed by modern industrialisation, by modern mechanisms, the new sciences and technologies, as well as by new evolutionary theories and the establishment of new religions, cults and beliefs. The period above all created new moral attitudes, thoroughly revising views about mind, matter and body. It was a period dominated by mood rather than by style. It stressed the importance of individual creativity and personal freedoms.

Although the term 'modern movement' was used by Mackintosh as early as 1901, it is, as I have said, more often associated with the 1920s and with the struggle that went on at that time in the arts – theatre and painting in particular – at the Bauhaus and in the USSR. Its importance as a continuing definition of contemporary housing, however, should not be ignored. Robert Hughes's television series, *The Shock of the New*, (as well as more reliable scholarly sources) have helped us to stress the importance of the term 'modern' as the only valid descriptive epithet of the whole period. It is sad to see its more recent misuse. ★

Hughes and others have recently tried to summarise the artistic aspirations of the second half of the nineteenth century through its own symbols. In the world of structure and imagery, this is perhaps best displayed in two remarkable engineering feats, Joseph Paxton's 1851 Crystal Palace in Hyde Park, and that memorable monument to single-minded modernism – created without a vestige of purpose other than that of symbolising the ingenuity of the modern engineering mind – Gustave Eiffel's great lattice-work Tower (299 metres tall), designed in 1887 but constructed for, and opened at, the Paris Exposition Universelle in 1889. Roland Barthes wrote in his brilliant essay 'The Eiffel Tower' that: 'Eiffel saw his tower in the form of a serious object, rational, useful, but men returned it to him in the form of a great Baroque dream.' This double meaning is profound. Barthes goes on: 'architecture is always dream and innovation, an expression of a Utopia, an instrument of convenience . . . At first it was sought to make the Tower into a temple of science – but this was only a metaphor. As a matter of fact the Tower is nothing so much as a kind of zero degree of the monument. It participates in no rite, in no cult . . . you cannot visit the Tower as a museum, there is nothing to see inside it.' In other words, like many architectural objects of the period, it was (and is) a myth. ★ And so, in a sense, is much of the domestic architecture of the period: the English house, like mulligatawny soup, is an invention – a mythology constructed by dreamers who fortunately were also supremely talented artists. They didn't call the circle of friends around Charles Rennie Mackintosh the Spook School for nothing!

Before we look at the nature of this domestic mythology in more detail, it may be worth remarking that, at the time of the opening of the Crystal Palace, the Prince Consort produced (along German lines) his well-designed artisans'

★This topical reference still has relevance. *See* Robert Hughes, *The Shock of the New*, Knopf, New York, 1981. Referring to the later International Style, Hughes speaks of its founders as Utopians whose 'very idea of Modernity signified a unique fusion of romance and rationality', p.167. Compare Barthes's view of Eiffel.

★Roland Barthes, *The Eiffel Tower and other Mythologies*, Hill and Wang, New York, 1979. All quotes from this edition, p.6ff.

houses. He commissioned models from Henry Roberts and others for workers' housing and flats, examples of which still remain (e.g. at Kennington Green in London and in Hertford). Such prototypes as these prefaced an urban housing programme for the working class which was later paralleled by a whole philanthropic programme of housing construction and improvement for the working classes, including the Peabody Settlement schemes and those that were motivated by what John Tarn has called 'the evangelical conscience'. Such urban developments, however, had little influence on the taste of the wealthy middle classes, the vulgarisation of which – particularly in furniture and furnishings – proved to be the disappointment of the Great Exhibition, which was noted for its designs 'in horse hair stuffing and papier mâché.' By the late 1850s, this vulgarity had invaded the interior of most middle-class homes. It induced over-decoration and created a profound fear, amongst normal mortals, of plain and unadorned surfaces. Everything that was not decorated was covered up, and a kind of historical pastiche, or eclecticism, was resorted to for exteriors.

The British architect and critic J.M. Brydon, writing in the *Architectural Association Notes* in 1901, suggested something of the confusion prevailing at the time:

'Another feature of the [nineteenth] century has been the eclecticism of many of our architects. Not only has a man worked in several styles (sometimes simultaneously) but he has done so in different phases of the same style, ringing the changes as it were in the search after novelty. This has become so marked towards the close of the century that we find hardly two men working in the same phase of any one style.'★

★J.M. Brydon, *AA Notes*, Vol. XVI, No. 167, 1901, in the article 'The Nineteenth Century', pp.1-5.

Brydon stressed, however, that the one great achievement of this period was the 'artistic regeneration of the English house.' His readers believed him. Like Muthesius, he understood that if there was one thing in which the English architects of the second half of the nineteenth century excelled it was in this area of domestic work. To quote him again:

'There are no more beautiful, comfortable and well planned modern homes in the world than are to be found in this England of ours, and none so characteristic of the country in which they are built, an artistic result which we owe in the main to the genius and influence of Mr Norman Shaw.'★

★Brydon, p.4.

Although these words were written a few years before the publication of *Das englische Haus*, Muthesius, too, had isolated Norman Shaw (1831-1912) as the foundation stone of the new architecture. Muthesius insisted that Shaw had 'carried the contemporary world with him.' He had, with his short-lived partner Eden Nesfield (1835–88), overwhelmed the architectural world with his achievements. Muthesius spoke of Shaw's great glass windows, which reflected the 'essence of the House', and Shaw's plans for English country houses recognised the basic philosophy that Muthesius believed in: functionalism – a more 'modern' term can hardly be found to suggest the allocation of specific areas or zones in planning domestic arrangements. This was a utilitarian matter devoid of ethical questions. Earlier, the architects and theorists of the Gothic Revival, especially A.W.N. Pugin, had felt that houses should reflect Christian principles and – to quote John Burnett's recent remark – 'follow the purposes and a social propriety ordained by God.'★ A kind of holy functionalism, if you like.

★John Burnett, *A Social History of Housing 1815-1970*, Methuen, London, 1980 (1978) p.109.

Pugin wrote: 'every person should be lodged as becomes his station and dignity, and in this there is nothing contrary to, but in accordance with, the Catholic principle.' As such, Christian justification for hierarchical housing, Burnett declares, was carried to extreme lengths in the work of Anglican architects, and certain signals were provided in this housing to indicate the status of the occupants. 'Privacy, respectability and distinctive social identification were the leading characteristics of the middle class houses.'★ Inside the house, the chief characteristics sought after were comfort and the accumulation of personal (or family) property: treasuries filled to overflowing with furniture, carpets, pictures, draperies, shelves, mirrors, ornamental objects and curiosities formed the essential ingredients of Victorian home life.

★Burnett, p.109.

Hermann and Anna Muthesius
taking tea at their house, The
Priory , Hammersmith, London,
c.1900.

*Burnett, p.111.

In a period of industrialisation and technology there was a total rejection of utilitarian values. Burnett calls it: 'solid comfort and a cosy clutter' in which 'Architecture in the proper sense of the word . . . was not a principal determinant of middle class house form.'* As it changed in the last third of the century – certainly for the enlightened client – architecture (and style) became of paramount importance. Instead of dealing with men like Mr Pooter, the architect found himself communicating ideas – innovatory or otherwise – to enlightened clients and an increasingly receptive public. The English house came into its own as a new, fresh concept. It was connected in a kind of theoretical relay race which saw the 'cosy and comforting' ideas gradually transformed over a period of time by the notion of the simple life uncluttered by superficial accumulations. Decorated objects were dropped, plain surfaces increased. Fundamental changes in domestic planning occurred, brought about by the introduction of new means of lighting, by plumbing and by the desire for a new spatial organisation in the home. William Morris declared: 'Have nothing in your home except what you know to be useful and believe to be beautiful.' It was Morris who advocated a return to the land and a return to nature. He led the socialist thrust towards peaceful reform which provided an anti-urban and anti-industrialist emphasis. The new middle-class domestic architecture was viewed in a sense as a product of the times. It embodied an antipathy on the part of its designers to the prevailing industrial culture. Many of the artistic and intellectual elite assumed a position that was entirely approved of by Hermann Muthesius who, in numerous books and articles on British architecture produced during his stay at the German Embassy in London from 1896 to 1903, was the only person to acknowledge the fundamental importance and nature of the domestic revolution.

Living close to nature formed the basis of much of the prevailing 'town planning' concepts of the time from Bedford Park at Turnham Green, London, in the 1870s to Ebenezer Howard's ideas in the mid 1890s for new garden cities expounded in his brilliant economic treatise, *Tomorrow, A Peaceful Path to Real Reform*, later published as *Garden Cities of Tomorrow* (1903). His central idea (learned earlier in USA) was that the size of towns could be consciously controlled. Letchworth was designed for about 30,000 people and Welwyn Garden City for 40,000.

Historians of the period have been strikingly ignorant of the close relationship between changes in town planning and house design. Even Muthesius appears not to have been aware of the close connection at the time of his study of the English house. Not until the 1960s, when Walter Creese prepared his study, *Search for Environment*, a comprehensive history of the Garden City Movement, was the relationship fully analysed outside the polemics created by the Garden City adherents themselves.

The return to nature and the land also inspired an interest in vernacular forms and hand craftsmanship. It inspired Philip Webb in the Red House for William Morris (1859) to think through such early 'modern' ideas as texture, orientation, the use of colour and native materials (which became fundamental in the Bauhaus course at Weimar), even though no bathroom was provided. He also pointed to new possibilities in planning and housing layout. But Morris himself soon moved on to Kelmscott (in 1871) and to a traditional manor house that offered him the freedom of rural life. There he nurtured his interests and developed his skills in mankind's prime craftsmanly interest, the printed word. There he absorbed himself, too, with the possibilities of the new socialist setup. There he lived out his own medieval myths.

Two years after the Red House was completed, William Richard Lethaby was born.★ His position is seen now as that of the indisputable catalyst of the period, as practitioner, theorist and later educationalist. It is necessary for me to dwell briefly on Lethaby here because of his interest in nature and its atavistic, esoteric and magical qualities. He initiated, admittedly in a rather wildly romantic way, a new interest in nature's structure and form, developing some ideas from James Fergusson's rude stones philosophy into profound and perceptive observations on architectural history. From 1892 onwards, Lethaby's ideas both surprised and stimulated a new generation of architects.

It may prove worthwhile for a moment to divert from the English house in order to investigate briefly the two backbone concepts that lie behind Lethaby's ideas: nature and reason. They both relate to my theme. Both were, for him, different aspects of symbolism. Behind all structure and form there are to be found 'the esoteric principles of architecture', as Lethaby called them, principles that are explained by reference to the changing conception of reality which, like nature, is in constant flux. Beauty in the Vitruvian sense was therefore, for Lethaby, relative. His theory suggests that the famous phrase '*Commoditie, firmness* and *delight*' might be rephrased as 'Utility, durability and nature', style in which 'Beauty may flow into the soul like a breeze!'

And as far as sweet reason goes, initially it was probably through the 'arts of construction' (a phrase much loved of Lethaby, C.F.A. Voysey and Raffles Davison, but probably attributable to Robert Kerr) that the idea of 'reasonable' or rational design could be seen – that quality which was recognised by Muthesius as functionalism. However, it was Paxton himself, that brilliant man of nature, who caused the world to gasp at the first major determined attempt to create a rational means of construction and a 'non style' utilitarian (building) architecture in 1851. He produced the world's largest single prefabricated structure (83,600 square metres of it) which, if not the first fully worked out example of modular construction, at least produced its most complex programme. It was built of 'rational' and revolutionary materials. In 1951 Christopher Hobhouse wrote: 'Glass was no more regarded in 1850 as a building material than alabaster is today.'★ The Crystal Palace required about one third of the annual glass production of the British Isles. Ruskin abhorred its utility, although he acknowledged its idealism. In 1857, he was exhorting London architects to erect a vast dome over London in similar materials.

At the outset, I referred to an iconoclastic critic, who with his sharp wit and his Scottish candour cut through the cant of his day. Robert Kerr was born in

★A useful essay on Lethaby and his relationship to Muthesius is to be found in Julius Posener, 'Muthesius in England', *From Schinkel to the Bauhaus*, AA Paper No. 5, London, 1972, pp.16-23. *See also* W.R. Lethaby, *Architecture, Nature and Magic*, Duckworth, London, 1956, and *Architecture, Mysticism and Myth*, Architectural Press, London, 1974. Muthesius called Lethaby's Central School (he was joint principal with George Frampton when it opened in 1896) 'probably the best run school in Europe'.

★Christopher Hobhouse, *1851 and the Crystal Palace*, John Murray, London, 1950 (1937), p.32.

13

*John Summerson, *Victorian Architecture in England: Four Studies in Evaluation*, Norton, New York, 1971 (1970), p.7ff. *See also* John Summerson, *The Architectural Association, 1847-1947*, London, 1947. In these lectures (Bampton Lectures, Columbia University, New York, 1968) Summerson records Kerr's interest in aligning himself with the 'idea of a contemporary architecture' an 'entirely new style based on new materials and new circumstances', No. 5, p.120.

Below: Charles Rennie Mackintosh. *Right:* Hermann Muthesius before being sent to England.

Aberdeen in 1823 and died in London in 1904. His importance as another catalyst of the new domestic architecture should not be underestimated. His views were widely read among his professional colleagues. John Summerson has consistently stressed his importance as a potent force behind domestic architecture in the second half of the nineteenth century. Although Kerr built only one fairly important city building and a few country houses and remained a rather dull designer, Summerson nonetheless records: 'His significance for us now is that he was a man of acute intelligence and exceptional eloquence . . .'* His ideas, often expressed in vivid phraseology, give us a clear picture of the attitudes and prejudices of the period. In the 1840s, as a young man, he proposed the setting up of a radical students' association which in 1847 became the Architectural Association. By then he had already been to the United States and was keen on American notions in design, particularly ideas on circulation. He abhorred the Vitruvian fuddy-duddies of the Institute of Architects, which he described as a 'concern run by crooked tradesmen and doting antiquarians for their mutual and largely dishonest amusement.' More importantly – and linked to that contempt – he lamented the current obsession with styles and with copyism. 'The nineteenth century', he wrote, 'has to have its own style appropriate to its new powers and its new materials,' and one must be able to test architecture 'by principles of nature and reason.'

But now let me return to Muthesius. I have already implied that the chief document of the period was his famous work *Das englische Haus* (Wasmuth, its publisher, was to swing the emphasis to the American scene with the first publication of Frank Lloyd Wright's work in Europe six years later, in 1910). *Das englische Haus* was reissued in 1908 in a second edition with the embossed title design which we believe was done by Mackintosh's sister-in-law, Frances MacNair. That this masterly and brilliant study remained untranslated for so many decades is an appalling omission on the part of English architectural historians. It underlines the fact that the London-centred English-speaking world was not really interested in a German view of its own domestic history

Margaret Macdonald
Mackintosh.

★I am indebted to Hermann
Muthesius's son Eckart
Muthesius for much of this
information. For more detail, *see*
The English House, London,
1979. Eckart Muthesius, a noted
architect himself, is the godson
of Charles Rennie Mackintosh.

★W.R. Lethaby, 'Modern
German Architecture . . .' in
Form in Civilisation, Oxford
University Press, London, 1957,
pp.78-85.

★Muthesius, p.10

★Muthesius, p.10

★Muthesius, pp.3-4

any more than it was interested in the work of the Glasgow 'Spook School'. That is very sad because there is no better architectural book in any language. Lethaby understood this, of course, and later apologised for the omission. Whilst one can sympathise with and probably understand the anti-German prejudice of the inter-war years, it is good to note that the enormous debt to Hermann Muthesius was finally honoured in 1980 with the publication of at least a truncated version of the original text.

Muthesius was the only person who adequately understood what was going on in Britain in the last quarter of the nineteenth century. He was a professional, an architect, who was not just paid in money but also rewarded with diplomatic prestige for the meticulous work he carried out between 1896-1903 as the cultural and technical attaché at the German Embassy in London. He was charged with the responsibility of investigating the new English developments in architecture, design and education. He was to find out how the English lived, and his work took him all over the country. We might well call Hermann Muthesius's mission for the Imperial German government cultural espionage, undertaken for a divided and backward country which had become a major power in the very same period of the nineteenth century that he was investigating. The Kaiser was particularly aware of the difference in culture that existed between Germany and Britain. On his frequent visits to the British court, he embarrassed the members of his own establishment by his 'criticisms' of their boorishness and by the introduction of some English habits of dress or behaviour.★ The Kaiser was personally responsible for Muthesius's mission. As Lethaby recorded in 1915, Muthesius became the historian (in German) of the English free architecture. 'All the architects who at that time did any building were investigated, studied, tabulated, and I must say, understood. Then, just as our English free building arrived, or at least very very nearly did, there came a timid reaction and the re-emergence of the catalogued styles.'★ This comment is significant. Not only was it written during the war but it acknowledged the veracity of Muthesius's history. Lethaby also recognised and understood that Muthesius had discovered in Britain a truly bourgeois (*bürgerlich*) society where the rich kept imitating their betters, the aristocracy. But as Muthesius wrote: 'The Englishman builds his house for himself alone . . . Nothing is further from his mind than a desire to impress other people with his house. Indeed, he avoids conspicuous features, showy architecture that might attract attention just as in his dress he shuns everything that might render him conspicuous. In the English house one would look in vain for the kind of pomposity that in Germany we are still devoted to.'★

Muthesius saw the whole new domestic movement in architecture, his English house style, as one which had for 40 years been pitted against the imitation of styles. It had, he claimed, been inspired by simple buildings in the country and had yielded splendid results. In Muthesius's view, it had a didactic purpose: 'The same reasonable straightforward attitude which informs the shape of the house can be seen in the way the house is placed on the ground and fits into the surrounding countryside. It adapts itself to nature and house and garden are treated as one closely integrated unit.'★ The English it seemed, did not live in cities!

In the preface to *Das englische Haus*, Muthesius acknowledges his own debt to the work of two predecessors: to the German Robert Dohme who published a work on the English House in 1888, and to Robert Kerr, whom we have already mentioned and who produced his remarkable book, *The Gentleman's House*, in 1861.★ It was during the quarter of a century between these two titles, Muthesius claims, that the great changes occurred in housing design; fifteen to twenty-five years that proved decisive in British architecture and in the later modern developments of the period in which the world witnessed the sensationally popular modernism of the Paris Expositions of 1889 and 1900, a period, indeed, that saw Modernism emerge as part of a Secessionist movement out of the inventive Art Nouveau and saw the creation of a whole school of independent designers following the precepts of Morris and Ruskin. Muthesius claims that the success of British architects after 1800 was due to the

Hermann and Anna Muthesius
taking tea in their garden.

fact that they broke with the styles of fine architecture. In other words, they broke the rules of the past, rules that had previously been unassailable. However, Muthesius went on, 'they did not achieve anything like artistic freedom . . .' and that's a very fine continental distinction for you, but one, as you think on it, that has a profound undertone.

So who were these architects whom Muthesius isolated as 'foundation stones' of the new architecture? To him the most important, as I have suggested, was his family friend Norman Shaw. Muthesius claimed that Shaw 'carried the contemporary world with him,' and that he and Eden Nesfield overwhelmed the architectural world with their achievements. Shaw's great glass windows reflected 'the essence of the house'. Muthesius recognised that the most important single achievement in domestic design was the creation of the Red House for William Morris by Philip Webb. Webb emerges as the first true adherent of the Arts and Crafts philosophy, however ill-defined that may have been in architctural terms. Among the first generation innovators, Muthesius also recognised the contribution made by John Douglas (the Chester architect), John Sedding, the very original and practical architect Ernest George, and by T.L. Collcutt. With the younger generation (his own age group) Muthesius established close personal contact and acted less like a critic and more like a promoter of new talent. He saw in C.F.A. Voysey, C.R. Ashbee, M.H. Baillie Scott, W.R. Lethaby and Charles Rennie Mackintosh the germination of a new style in architecture: they could be claimed as pioneers of the new domestic architecture. They were his heroes and his discoveries, to be promoted among his own folk.

We cannot here investigate the abundant detail of Herr Muthesius's monumental work. It should be sufficient to recall that the book covers the work of all the significant British architects of the period. With German scholarly fastidiousness, the record is never dull, never short on relevant comment and always unambiguous as it grapples with what Julius Posener has referred to as the 'English mood of the moment' – because English theory at the time was never as consistent as Muthesius's own theories. The mood was against styles. It was anti-Italian, anti-Renaissance and in favour, as we have already hinted, of an architecture related to nature and most precisely to the relevance of its own age. The theory at the commencement of the new movement was to be found in Pugin's writings with their quasi-theological basis, in Ruskin's most rhetorical periods and in its 'true form' – 'free from the Ruskinian alloy', as Posener puts it – as it appears in Lethaby's wide-ranging writings. Lethaby was an almost exact contemporary of Muthesius. In his turn, he later recalled, in *Form in Civilisation*, that the architecture of the period he had lived through was one of adventure, moved by the spirit of experiment.★ His straightforward English thinking excited Muthesius and one can understand why. What other critic could have brushed that whole theoretical and historical period off in a paragraph (and I use Posener's translation back into English!): 'Ruskin, he was cracked on *Seven Lamps*; Morris, he was only the arts and craftsman who did not know about the majesty and the wonderful occult essence of architecture. March Philips thinks architecture should have something to do with life, which clearly it has not. Archer, Wells and Clutton Brock, they are only literature men, Muirhead Bone and Pennell mere sketchers. Fergusson in his way was continually preaching the doctrine that architects would be astonished to find how easy it was to do right, and how difficult to do wrong when expressing the truth.'★ Robert Kerr, of course, he recognised as a critic of ability who had provided the seeds of the 'new free architecture'. Muthesius recognised that the Morrisian Arts and Crafts movement and the free architecture movement had in fact little to do with one another and he reminded his readers that Sedding was the only direct contact with the Arts and Crafts movement itself. Philip Webb, he acknowledged, was involved in both. Neither movement really came to terms with the deeply rooted history of the English house, and certainly neither of them was concerned in its re-evaluation. That was left to the individual architects whom Muthesius cites amongst his innovators, the chief of them being Mackintosh, that profoundly human soul whose work was by no means confined to domestic design but whose sensibility, mythologising and practicality Muthesius acknowledges. Mackintosh perhaps should have the last word, albeit quoting J.D. Sedding: 'There is hope in honest error, none in the icy perfections of the mere stylist.'★ But, ironically perhaps, it was Peter Behrens in Germany and others who were to benefit from the profundities of change brought about by the revolution in the British house.

★W.R. Lethaby, *Form in Civilisation. See* the essay 'Architecture as Form in Civilisation', pp.1–13.

★Posener, *From Schinkel to the Bauhaus*, pp.18–19.

★Muthesius records his own impressions of Mackintosh's early work in *The English House*, pp.51–54. For a more detailed account of their personal connections, *see* N. Jopek, 'Mackintosh und Muthesius' in *Jahrbuch der Hamburger Kunstsammlungen*, Vol. 24, 1979, pp.151–158.

Anna and Hermann Muthesius in the living room of their house The Priory, Hammersmith, c.1900.

LETHABY AS A KEY
TO MACKINTOSH

Robert Macleod

There cannot be any single key to open that Pandora's Box of architectural surprises, the work of Mackintosh. Nor can W.R. Lethaby be seen as a primary visual or formal influence on Mackintosh, although there appears to be at least one instance in which this was the case. It is principally in the realm of ideas and attitudes that the work of Lethaby is important to an understanding of the architecture of Mackintosh.

Lethaby is one of those figures who always appear in any inquiry into the period around the turn of the century: hugely respected both by his peers and by subsequent historians, but hardly ever read and, I would suggest, even less understood, in spite of his constant attempts to explain himself and to redirect the forces of his own generation.

He was born at Barnstaple in Devon in 1857, the son of a carver, gilder and framemaker. After leaving school at the age of fourteen he was articled to a local architect, Alexander Lauder, whence he proceeded, briefly by way of Derby, to Norman Shaw's office in London in 1879. He remained with Shaw until 1892, by which time he had been Shaw's Principal Assistant for some years and had had a substantial impact on the form and character of many of Shaw's major buildings of the period. During the 1880s, he was engaged in a rich variety of activities and projects which established the most important influences in his life, among them his close and continuing friendships with William Morris and, in particular, Philip Webb.

In 1892, he established an architectural practice on his own account and continued to practise until 1904, when he stopped for the expressed reason that he felt he did not have the technical skills or even the heart to meet the challenges of the twentieth century. It was an honourable choice, but one that could be seen as more appropriate to many other architects, then and now, than to Lethaby.

In 1892, Lethaby published his first independent book, *Architecture, Mysticism and Myth*. As far as one can gauge from this distance, and from the recorded comments of such friends as Reginald Blomfield, the book was both impressive and utterly baffling to his contemporaries.

Towards the end of his life, Lethaby undertook the extraordinary task of re-writing the entire book from fresh sources, as a series of articles for *The Builder* magazine. It was published posthumously in one volume under the title *Architecture, Nature and Magic*. In the rewritten edition, Lethaby described the original undertaking as a 'thesis that the development of building practice and ideas of the world structure acted and reacted on one another,' that 'Nature was . . . the source of much of what is called architectural decoration in a way which is not recognised in the histories,' and that 'thought of magical properties generally had a very wide and deep influence on the development of ancient building customs.'

In other words, he was conducting an inquiry into the very origins of meaning in architecture, into the phenomenon of style. It was an immense undertaking, as he himself acknowledged, and yet one which he felt had essential practical consequences for his own time. In the later version he said:

'What will here concern us are some realities behind the phenomena of structure and the appearances of styles. Such an inquiry, remote as it may seem, will be of some immediate practical consequence for us, for in the result we may recognise that there is, and must be, an impassable gulf between all ancient

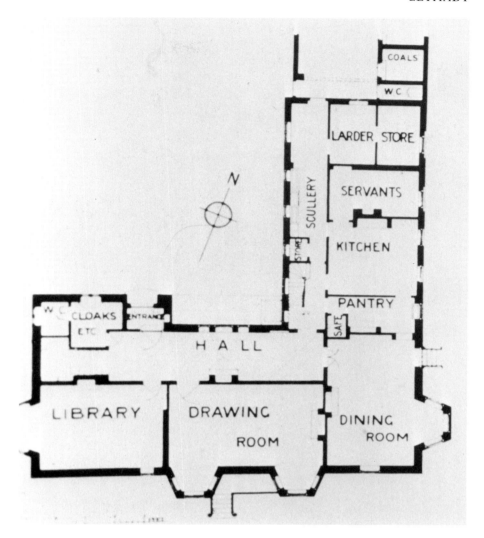

The Hurst, Sutton Coldfield, 1893. Plan of ground floor. This plan is very close to that of Windyhill, and of its successor, The Hill House. In the case of Windyhill, a square garden pond with cypresses at each corner, which Lethaby used at some distance from his house, reappears at Windyhill in the north courtyard. From *The Modern Country House*, c.1910–12.

W.R. Lethaby

arts and our own. At the inner heart of ancient building were wonder, magic, and symbolism; the motive of ours must be human service, intelligible structure, and verifiable science.'

If the book in its original form remained a mystery to most of Lethaby's contemporaries, one architect at least made an instant response. Mackintosh gave a lecture in February 1893 to, it is now thought, students at the Glasgow School of Art. A very substantial portion of the Mackintosh lecture was direct plagiarism from the Lethaby book – even to the adaptation of Lethaby's slightly apologetic introduction to the book as his own introduction to his lecture!

The important issue for us, however, is how immediately Mackintosh leapt on the issues with which Lethaby was grappling. It can, I believe, be argued that much of Mackintosh's subsequent building can be seen as an attempt to work out in visual terms many of the concerns with which Lethaby was engaged.

One of the curious aspects of Lethaby and, it must be said, one of the characteristics which make it even more difficult for us to come to terms with him as an architect and theorist is that he never apparently attempted to do this himself: he never attempted, except in the most ambiguous and subtle way, to give visual images to his own ideas. Almost certainly, the overriding reason for this diffidence – if it may be so called – was that the very esssence of his message was that 'a new style' was not what was needed, and that if he were to attempt to develop visually the consequences of his own thinking, the result would almost certainly be labelled with a stylistic identity and the core of his

The Hurst, from the south west.

message, which had to do with approach and priorities, would be irrevocably overwhelmed.

There are some pieces of evidences to support this idea. In his final building, Brockhampton Church of 1904, which was built by direct labour from the parish and neighbourhood, Lethaby designed the main structure as a series of low-sprung, 'Gothic' arches built of a local stone in a traditional manner, supporting a shell of *in situ* poured concrete (with the boarding pattern of the shuttering exposed to the interior) and then covered by local thatching. The total ensemble thus provided 'point loading' of a known and determinate kind, economical and fireproof enclosure, and a combination of weatherproofing and insulation. But it did not provide any readily identifiable image or form for the future.

What, then, were the issues with which Lethaby was engaged? He was first of all drawing directly on the teachings and writings of his friends William Morris and Philip Webb. It is worth noting here that the theories which are attributed to Morris were deeply and inseparably bound up with those of the less articulate Webb.

To understand the ideas about architecture that were promulgated by Morris and Webb, it is necessary to go back to what I have elsewhere called the serious phase of the Gothic Revival, beginning with A.W.N. Pugin's *Contrasts* of 1836. This book and the later volume, *True Principles of Pointed or Christian Architecture*, established the quite revolutionary idea, which has since become a common-place, that there was a causal relationship between a society's art and artefacts and its essential nature. Inevitably, in the thinking of Pugin and his Gothic Revival followers, ethical judgments about the nature of society became inextricably mingled with aesthetic ones about the value of its artefacts. Although we might find Pugin's particular judgements, at the least, bizarre and the thesis historically untenable, there can be little doubt that such notions as the intrinsic rightness of functional expression and the very term 'honest detailing' spring directly from this beginning.

The connection of these ideas with those of the Arts and Crafts movement is direct, but with a fundamental difference. Where the Gothic Revivalists saw the theological bases of the medieval period as the foundation for art and form in the inspiration and authority that was channelled through the church, the Arts and Crafts apologists had their medieval models in the guilds. The medieval guilds provided the inspiration for Morris's brand of socialism, and, more particularly for our purposes, the model for his vision of art founded in craft.

This switch, from theology to craft, meant for Morris and Webb directing attention in a quite unprecedented way from the form and style of buildings to the way in which they went together. When Philip Webb began independent architectural practice, his first commission was the Red House for William Morris. Although his house has received an extraordinary amount of attention from historians, it was in fact almost wholly derived in its salient characteristics from the typical country parsonages of William Butterfield. Webb held Butterfield in the highest respect for the whole of his working life, in spite of his own dissociation from the firmly Gothic Revival premises that directed the older man.

But in their attention to the Red House, historians have too often overlooked the later body of Webb's work which was of such enormous influence on the following generation, not least on Lethaby. As Webb's design progressed, so his references became richer and, it must be said, more ambiguous. What is too seldom noticed is the rich and diverse eclecticism that formed the Arts and Crafts movement. Webb acknowledged this and described the way in which his friend Morris used this diversity of source, noting how, wherever something may have originated, a 'sea-change' came over it on landing. As it was with Morris, so it was with Webb himself, but with each of his importations the fundamental transformations occurred by the loving adaptation of 'foreign' forms to English materials and ways of building. These were the ultimate generators of form and style.

William Morris had confessed to a fundamental lack of interest in science and metaphysics – he was, in his own words, 'careless of both'. Lethaby was emphatically interested in both, and it was with respect to these two issues, perhaps more than to anything else, that he can be seen to have brought the thinking of his mentors and friends forward to the new century.

In his early study, *Architecture, Mysticism and Myth*, the emphasis on science and metaphysics is evident from the beginning. Indeed, the principle of 'building practice and ideas of the world structure' acting and reacting on one another to create style was the essence of the book. However, unlike Webb, for whom building practice and a happy eclecticism could combine to lay the foundations for what has become known as the 'English Free Style', Lethaby sought a purer metaphysic. Alas, it could not be. In his own words towards the end of his life: 'the ages of magic crafts have passed and the only mysteries left to building are the true mystery of reality, and the other strange mystery that directors of building can be so silly as to practise the sham styles and provide whim-works.'

All Saints Church, Brockhampton, 1902, from the south.

Lethaby had begun with the Arts and Crafts premise about the nature of art, that is, that craft, be it the craft of building or anything else, could be elevated to the level of art. The heart of art, therefore, lay in work. 'Art is the expression of man's joy in labour' and many such expressions constantly reiterated the emphasis on work. Indeed, Lethaby said: 'Man cannot be civilised or remain civilised by what he does in his spare time, only by what he does as his work.'

But here the Arts and Crafts movement came up against a basic and un-avoidable dilemma of its time. That in a period of industrialisation, hand work was extremely expensive. The only people who could afford the craft work of Morris and his friends were the wealthy, although the fundamental intention of this work was to create a new, socially based 'folk' art. Morris expressed the difficulty succinctly when he was in a rage and was asked what was wrong: 'It is only that I spend my life in ministering to the swinish luxury of the rich.'

If this was a general dilemma of the Arts and Crafts movement, it was a very specific architectural one as well. Just as hand labour was expensive, so would be the release into 'creativity' of each of the workmen on a building site. Thus to achieve the kind of loving hand quality that characterised the best of humble traditional building, much more autocratic control by the designer had to be exercised, and, paradoxically, the ordinary freedom of the workmen had to be severely curtailed.

Webb the Socialist, and Lethaby after him, inevitably worked for the wealthy; their country houses, which we so much admire, cost between £20,000 and £40,000 when a detached three-bedroom cottage could be built for £100 to £200. The architects could hardly be said to be addressing the ordinary heart of what we now call the 'built environment'.

What they did do, however, was to build well and to bring the 'science' of building to the heart of design. The result was that, in the generation between 1890 and World War I the building quality of the better houses reached a level never previously matched and, with the unsurpassed availability of good quality material and skilled workmanship, has probably never been equalled since.

However, the other important point to note about these buildings is that they could provide no models for the larger commercial, industrial and in-stitutional buildings increasingly demanded by the society of their time. The loving attention to traditional materials, to craft traditions and to uncompro-mising quality could find no place in these larger, generally urban, challenges, nor could the available budgets cope. Neither could there be the same identi-fication of the man with his labour. With a large steel-framed building, who is the individual who can identify with the quality of his work in the way that, say, a traditional bricklayer still could? Was it the maker of the steel, or the off-site fabricator, or the crane-driver, or the riveter or welder? In the increasingly fragmented and articulated processes invoked by large-scale modern building, each element of labour, except for, of course, the all-seeing, overseeing eye of the designer, became more and more detached from the specific nature of the end product.

This was a problem with which Lethaby grappled throughout his life and never resolved. Yet he did bring to it an increasingly clear view of what was needed and was not being supplied. He declared, at the first Board of Edu-cation of the Royal Institute of British Architects, that Schools of Architecture must become Schools of Building Science. This, incidentally, is the first use that I have yet found of the term in a formal sense; it was clearly unfamiliar to his contemporaries, for the surviving minute notes that this is 'Professor Lethaby's term'. His view, as expressed increasingly towards the end of his life was that the new materials and methods of building must be understood, mastered and used so that out of the new rationality and the new science would eventually come the new mysteries of the world, what he called the 'true mysteries of reality', the mysteries of 'service and science'.

It is possible that in reading these words superficially, one might imagine Lethaby as a true pioneer of the Modern Movement as it emerged later in the century. This was emphatically not the case, for he lived long enough to see it and to comment on it. In 1929, lecturing at the Architectural Association, he

All Saints Church,
Brockhampton: the nave.

said: '. . . a sense of pure construction on an intelligible basis would be an anchor-age against a present-day eddy of setting up "Modernism" as a *style*, instead of seeking the truly modern, which expands and forms itself . . . M. Corbusier has called houses "machines to live in", and the thought is suggestive; but a reasonable building is not necessarily a series of boxes or a structure of steel. The most scientific and sensible building for given conditions might still be of brick and thatch.' He saw in the Modern Movement an essential ambiguity – that, while it purported to reflect a kind of rationalism and to embody the 'science' of the day, it did so in visual, that is to say, *stylistic* terms, and not in its reality. He went on to say: 'At once I felt that they should be described as in "Ye olde modernist style". That is the point: this "modernism" is regarded as a style, whereas being truly modern would be simply right and reasonable.'

The path of the *right* and the *reasonable* is rather cold fare to offer – architects can become terribly tied up with their images. But Lethaby, of course, was containing in that simple proposition a rich and diverse range of rights and reasonablenesses: the reverence and respectful emulation of the old, the grace-ful acceptance of the new, the free and flexible response to the real, the love of the way things went together. With all of these and more, there is no doubt that Mackintosh was in full accord. But although they had one significant friend in common, there is no record of their ever having met or exchanged ideas. This is a particular tragedy, for it can be argued that in much of his work Mack-intosh was giving strong and topical vision to the thinking of Lethaby.

There is perhaps one further issue with which Lethaby was primarily con-cerned and which had an important bearing on the life and work of Mackintosh. In 1896 Lethaby had been appointed first principal of the Central School of Arts and Crafts in London. In the course of his career there he was responsible for establishing a craft-based education which formed an important model for Art School education in Britain and Europe. He carried the work further as Professor of Design at the Royal College of Art. He was a natural choice, there-fore, as a founding member of the Board of Education of the Royal Institute of British Architects. But his plea for a kind of architectural education radically different from the one proposed fell on deaf or unsympathetic ears.

It is not generally realised how late and how narrow was the development of tertiary – and even of secondary – education in England. Matthew Arnold,

Oxford Professor of Poetry and H.M. Inspector of Schools, was one of the great pioneers of the development of education in the nineteenth century, but although he did much for its establishment he did little for its breadth of vision. He expressed a view of culture as 'sweetness and light' from which training for specific functional roles in society was clearly excluded. It was a view that was increasingly reinforced through the second half of the nineteenth century, the exact period when architects, principally through the R.I.B.A., were attempting not only to establish the profession formally but to enhance its status by making it a subject for university education. Towards the end of the century, two universities established chairs of architecture, Liverpool and University College, London. At the same time, as colleges of art and other institutions increasingly provided formal education for prospective architects, the informal and often casual system of articling and apprenticeship began to lose dominance.

However, the bringing of architecture into the classroom did not, as Lethaby would have it, move it into the laboratory and workshop, but instead transported it into the academic *atelier*, or something modelled on that tradition. It was the system of the Ecole des Beaux Arts that was the main historical prototype, and by far the most influential one, for most of the western world, including America.

The result was inevitable. In place of the loose romanticism of the 'artists' or the close involvement with building craft of the Lethabites, there rose a new/old academic classicism of the kind familiar in France, but until then the very rare exception in England. Edwardian architecture, with its British Empire veneer on its French neoclassical bones, was born. Its beginnings can be seen in the 'nineties, and by World War I it was a force to be reckoned with; after the hiatus of the war, it swept all before it, subsiding into the paler neo-Georgian and finally being ousted by the Modern Movement.

Lethaby, with all his educational achievement, could not fight both the aspirations of his establishment-oriented contemporaries and all the perceptions of the English middle classes as to what truly constituted culture. The real architectural victims were a generation of deeply committed architects for whom Lethaby was a central spokesman and Mackintosh a great visionary, for only rare exceptions among that remarkably promising generation were to find anything like adequate architectural opportunities again.

There are, it must be said, stirrings of their kind of thinking again in the aftermath of the fragmentation of the Modern Movement. What they will become remains to be seen. What we lost cannot be measured, but there is no doubt that in the work, thinking and writing of Lethaby and Mackintosh lay the seeds of a modern movement that might have been.

Perspective of Liverpool Cathedral competition entry, 1902. This was a design by a group of architects and artist led by Lethaby, in which his hand was clearly predominant. It was to have been a massive loadbearing concrete structure.

MACKINTOSH IN CONTEXT

Andrew MacMillan

Charles Rennie Mackintosh was perhaps the most remarkable architect to emerge in Britain at the turn of the century, and certainly the only one personally to influence the development of the Modern Movement. Around 1900, he was able to display to an astonished Europe an opus of outstanding clarity and versatility incorporating the design not only of buildings but also of their entire contents, furniture and furnishings, textiles and crockery, even floral decorations. He was also a prolific graphic designer, draughtsman and painter of exceptional calibre.

His greatest domestic building, The Hill House in Helensburgh, could be seen as either the purest masterpiece of the English House movement or the finest Scottish Baronial house of the Edwardian era. Equally, in the Glasgow School of Art, Mackintosh could be said to have created the finest public building of the English Free School or the first genuine monument of the European Modern Movement.

Both alternatives are indicative of Mackintosh's ambiguous stature and place in history and raise fundamental questions about him. Accused in his own lifetime of partiality for strange foreign notions emanating from Germany or France or even Japan, where did Mackintosh really stand? From where was his vision derived? Where did he want to go? And, fundamentally, what was his real achievement?

Mackintosh was one of that European generation of architects, the 'bright young men' of 1890-1910, whose individual desire to create a new national architecture was widely enough spread to be thought of as a new International movement. Antoni Gaudí in Spain, Otto Wagner and Josef Hoffmann in Vienna, Victor Horta and Hector Guimard in France and Belgium, Frank Lloyd Wright in America were all ostensibly interested in reviving, re-vamping or even inventing an appropriate national style. I say 'inventing' particularly in the case of Wright, because Wright wanted to cast off the European 'colonial' tradition and instead create a 'Prairie style' of architecture appropriate to the prairies of his homeland, – a Usonian architecture, as he was later to term it.

Having observed that this nationalist tendency was manifest internationally, I propose to examine it through a case study, as it were, of Charles Rennie Mackintosh. Not only does his work offer a good individual example of the

The Hill House, Helensburgh, can be seen as either the purest masterpiece of the English House school or the finest baronial house of the Edwardian era.

general phenomenon, but it also shows how a place-specific approach led to the eliciting of general principles which were to inform and engender a genuine new 'International' style from the shared cultural and industrial base of the twentieth century.

I want first to examine his training and education, and how that had a bearing upon his philosophies and his beliefs about style, then to look at the evidence for his interest in a 'Scottish' architecture. I want, too, to look at some other common catalytic experiences that his generation shared: the English House movement, the arts of Japan, and the impact of the illustrated art magazine after the invention of photomechanical reproduction.

Mackintosh's architectural education was that of a typical late Victorian architect in the period immediately before the standardisation of education throughout Europe and America in a Beaux-Arts mould.

In 1884, at the age of sixteen, he entered into an apprenticeship in the office of John Hutchinson, a Glasgow architect. In that office, for the next five years, he obtained a practical training and a professional orientation, and, having enrolled in evening classes on the advice of the chief assistant, he also attended a formal course of study in Architecture and Building.

Mackintosh had an extremely successful school career. He was awarded a number of school prizes in 1885, 1886 and 1888, two National Institute prizes in 1887, the Institute Bronze medal in 1888, and one of the Queen's Prizes in 1889.

Having completed his apprenticeship in 1889, he moved to the office of Honeyman & Keppie, continuing both to follow his course of study and to win awards. In 1890, he was awarded the Design Prize and the Greek Thomson Travelling Scholarship of the Glasgow Institute of Architects in addition to several School of Art prizes, and, in 1891, the Silver Medal of the Kensington Institute was awarded to him for his project for a Science and Art Museum, a design remarkably similar to that for Milwaukee State Library and Museum (1894) by his American contemporary Frank Lloyd Wright. In 1892, he finally gained the Gold Medal to complete his national medal hat trick.

His school drawings display both the classical bias of his education and the development of his skill as a draughtsman under the tutelage of Alexander 'Sandy' McGibbon, his drawing professor in the School of Art. The drawings also illustrate the nature of the Victorian course, the teaching of theory by the

The east end of Queen's Cross Church – a Scottish vision and the Victorian reality.

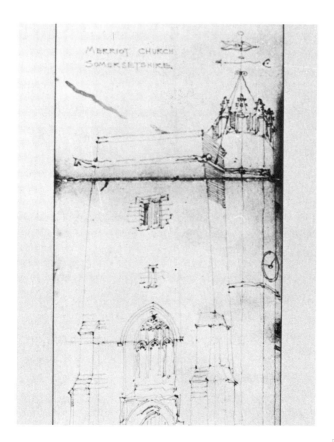

The drawing of Merriot Church in the sketchbook (*above*) clearly indicates the genesis of Queen's Cross Church (*right*).

study of historical models, the study of detail and ornament by drawing from plaster casts of selected fragments, and a marked preference for monumental public building in the design projects. Through the success of his schoolwork and the publication of his prize-winning projects in the professional press, Mackintosh was brought to the attention of his contemporaries in Glasgow and attracted minor national notice as a name to be watched.

His architectural aims can be seen emerging in his office work in an early perspective, his drawing for the Glasgow Herald Building (1894). Worked up from preliminary sketches in his Italian sketchbook, it is superficially classical in style but nevertheless already displays Mackintosh's characteristic plasticity, and an element of Scottish baronial architecture has begun to appear.

By the time of the drawing for the Martyrs' Public School (1896), Mackintosh was already not only using personal elements, particularly the staircase tower and the design of ventilators on the roof (also used on the Pettigrew building's dome, now to be seen in the gardens of The Hill House), but the superimposition of characteristic Scottish elements on the adjoining buildings indicates quite clearly a desire to 'Scottify', the existing tenement surrounding, as a comparison with the actual building will show.

This tendency is strikingly echoed in the contemporary Queen's Cross Church perspective. This drawing is less noteworthy for the building (which does not reach the same heights of innovation as Mackintosh's domestic or school work) than for the 'Mackintoshing' of the surroundings, which incorporate details from his recently designed School of Art, incidentally heavily borrowed from C.F.A. Voysey, as well as a few inventive Scottish vernacular transformations of the existing buildings. Again, a borrowing from his own sketchbooks (Merriot Church) is obvious and demonstrates the Victorian dependence on observed precedent in design.

These perspectives show how convincingly Mackintosh synthesised his classical training, his admiration of Voysey and the English School, his desire for a Scottish architecture and the observations contained in his notebooks.

Comparison of the windows and chimneys of a traditional house in Leith Walk with those at Windyhill reveals Mackintosh's appreciation of the nature of Scottish vernacular architecture.

In common with his international peer group, Mackintosh was learning the elements of architecture in a school at the same time as absorbing a practical ethos in a professional office.

His office was located in a city where industrial innovation and energy were perhaps at their most concentrated in the British Empire – as Barcelona was for Gaudí, Brussels for Horta and Guimard, and Chicago for Wright. Here the newest discoveries and techniques of servicing and construction were daily being put into practice. Plate glass, steel and cast iron, fireproof concrete, central heating, ventilation, drainage, gas and electric lighting were all undergoing research and development.

All this existed matter-of-factly alongside the routine application of the traditional canons of Classical architecture, used straight or translated to masquerade as Gothic (revival) architecture. But like many of his generation, as his perspectives show, Mackintosh had begun questioning those canons.

He came under the influence of Voysey through the medium of the newly published magazine, *The Studio*, and, travelling south, undertook a careful personal study of the contemporary English house, also making many detailed sketches with working notes of traditional English vernacular houses. What he then seemed to be doing was in effect adopting the English Free School movement and utilising it with Scottish details.

By this time, however, the English School, a splendid game for Edwin Lutyens, a cosy vocabulary for others, had degenerated into little more than a picturesque revival. Mackintosh went on in his own way to develop the movement's ideas and extend them significantly.

Hermann Muthesius, whose book on the English House was influential in Europe, appreciated his originality and his contribution to the continuing development of the English House movement thus:

'The London movement made its position clear: it would in future take no part in furthering the new ideas, a stance it has steadfastly maintained since the death of William Morris in 1896 until the present day. Not only, however, did the Scots (Mackintosh and his group) receive the liveliest recognition on the Continent from the moment they appeared there, but they had a seminal influence on the emerging new vocabulary of forms, especially and most continuously in Vienna, where an unbreakable bond was forged between them and the leaders of the Vienna movement over England's head.'

Perceptively, he also noted of the Four's work that:

'The central aim of these members is the room as work of art, as a unified organic whole, embracing colour, form and atmosphere. Starting from this notion they develop not only the room but the whole house, the sole purpose of the exterior of which is to enclose the rooms, their central concern, without laying any particular claim to an artistic appearance itself. Nevertheless Mackintosh with his strong architectonic sense sees to it that proper architectonic values are maintained here too; and his ground-plans are models of practicality and comfortable, convenient planning.'

Mackintosh's writings of this period, notably his paper on the Scottish Baronial style delivered to the Glasgow Art Association in 1891, still emphasise his belief in the need for a return to the Scottish native tradition. They also reveal his dependence for a general theory upon the writings of W.R. Lethaby. But as both his writings and the sketchbooks show, he had not merely emulated the forms of vernacular building as 'appropriate' in a national style, he also understood their genesis and recognised their social and tectonic relevance to a new architecture for his time.

Mackintosh's rejection of traditional historical European prototypes and his belief that a new 'contemporary' architecture would evolve from a study of national building characteristics link him with many other pioneers of around 1900 who also independently felt that nationalism would creatively substitute for historicism as a stimulus to design. Gaudí, Guimard and Wright were perhaps the clearest foreign exponents of this belief, which of course ultimately derived from Ruskin and the English School.

But as indicated already, this approach had degenerated in England into another kind of picturesque historicism, and the Englishness of English architecture had become the aim which led Lutyens and his generation to the so-called 'Wrenaissance', a national historicism rather than a derivation of architectural principle from a national way of building.

The next necessary step in the development of a genuine modern architecture required one more element for a genuine liberation from the past. And that catalyst was already there to be seen in the new illustrated art magazines: Japan.

Japanese art and architecture was known in Glasgow art circles; Japanese prints were available and popular; Glasgow artists had gone to Japan to paint the contemporary scene there; a Japanese house had been built at the International

Mackintosh's drawing of witch hazel is clearly influenced by the background of the Japanese print, like the middle picture on his living room mantelpiece.

Exhibition in Glasgow and Christopher Dresser of Glasgow had written his great catalogue of Japanese art.

In the 1890s, Glasgow, like Barcelona and Chicago, was a town of wealthy *nouveau riche* patrons, sympathetic to and supportive of contemporary art and artists. The work of the Glasgow School of painters in the 1880s, the later visit of the Hornel brothers to Japan and the acquisition and exhibition of the works of Whistler, Van Gogh and the French Impressionists by Glasgow dealers and collectors like Reid and Burrell: all these factors made the influence of Japanese art familiar to Mackintosh through his involvement in the affairs of a great school of art, for which he was currently designing new accommodation.

But there was more to it for Mackintosh than novelty. Japanese architecture revealed to him – as to Wright – that beyond the Picturesque and the Arts and Crafts there could be a true non-historical style based only on space and a direct use of material.

A glance at the photographs of Mackintosh's flat in Mains Street makes clear the extent to which Mackintosh was in possession of artefacts and prints from Japan, and a comparison of his flower drawings and some of the prints he owned make only too clear how vital the influence of Japan was on him.

The Japanese approach to the use of void, of negative ground in the prints (the *amor vacuii* as Madsen calls it), the use of flat bright areas of colour and, in particular, the exploitation of the material in the artistic act of transformation were sympathetic to concepts of modern living, and perhaps particularly to modern ideas of hygiene, an increasing use of glass, and the enjoyment by the urbanite of the pleasures of nature, sunshine and greenery.

It is interesting that only Mackintosh and Wright grasped the essence of space in the Japanese print, the use of interlocking ground and figure, rather than the line, which both increasingly rejected in their development. The Europeans, Horta, Guimard and H.C. Van de Velde stressed the value of the line and merely distorted the building form, producing a more whimsical, personal ornament and a short-lived architecture.

While continental architects were also stimulated by the discovery of a consistent art style which owed nothing to any historical European tradition, Mackintosh and Wright grasped its essential trait and saw the art forms for what they were in terms of making and representing space. Here the influence of John Ruskin and Philip Webb and Norman Shaw *et al.* in Britain and America had clearly set the scene for a deeper understanding and appreciation of what the study of Japan revealed.

Where Wright's immediate influences were Richardson out of Shaw, Mackintosh started by emulating Voysey (probably out of Webb). He had seen photographs of Voysey's works and from *The Studio* knew his drawings with their nervous line deriving from Beardsley's interpretation of the Japanese print.

It cannot be over-emphasised how much the newly invented photomechanical half-tone reproduction for printing affected the development of modern architecture by making contemporary architecture quickly available for evaluation throughout the world. And *The Studio* magazine, dominated by the English Arts and Crafts, was a prime example of such influence.

But Mackintosh, although receptive to and stimulated by the influence of Japan, was an architect in a great industrial city (not an administrative capital), where the potential of the machine was demonstrated. Thus, he developed an architecture well beyond that of Voysey, rose to international stature and influenced the subsequent development of the modern architecture of the heroic period.

What then was his achievement in the early years of the twentieth century? By 1900, he could demonstrate not only a substantial built opus but also an equally impressive portfolio of graphic and competition work. He could offer his peers in Europe a convincing model of an appropriate total architecture for modern times which was:

—non-historical, derived from the process of building, determined by use and

Guimard's gate at Castel Béranger shows the influence of Japanese line on European Art Nouveau.

responsive to context; capable of both monumentality and whimsy, yet not capricious

—absorbing and demonstrating the full potential of the new technologies of glass, steel and concrete; served by the new means and concepts of environmental control, gas and electric lighting and power, hot water and warm air heating

—manifesting a decorated construction and a constructed decoration; non-handcraft, utilising the potential of the machine

—an architecture of simple forms, uniquely shaped by a poetic insight into the existential nature of building, subject to an overriding control of extraordinary assurance and intellectual depth.

His vision supported the intuitions and approach of the early European pioneers and prepared the way for the later influences of Wright and Corbusier. Their work confirmed Mackintosh's revelations, displaying similar characteristics and a further extension of the architectural possibilities inherent in the abstraction of the building and in the employment of the machine in the building process.

Mackintosh's work can now be seen to have provided a necessary bridge between the old and the new at the turn of the century. His search for a new and appropriate architecture was informed both by personal analysis of organic and vernacular form and by his involvement in the day-to-day practice of architecture at a time of great social change and continuing technical innovation.

In re-appraisal, the three major aspects of his work can now be clearly perceived to belong in the main line of the evolution of the historical Modern Movement.

First, his rediscovery of the programmatic derivation of vernacular form and its application to architectural design as a general principle; the conditioning of building form by the interaction of use and technique. This was the essential principle of the heroic period, quite different from either the earlier, nineteenth-century historicist use of canonic form or the later picturesque use of vernacular compositions.

Second, his appreciation of the need to produce an appropriate total environment for modern life, which could accept current innovations in hygiene and technology, and utilise the potential of the machine as an inevitable replacement for handicraft. This made him an appropriate prophet in Europe for the revelations of Wright, which so conclusively directed the nature of the European experience after the publication of the Wasmuth monograph and separated him clearly from the self-indulgence of the English Arts and Crafts Movement. Mackintosh's importance as a designer and the extraordinary power of his furniture lies in the fact that he was the first serious furniture designer of the Machine Age. It is not by accident that shape not craft is the essence of product design: Mackintosh's furniture is now better made by modern machinery and glues and its iconic power enhanced.

Third, and herein lies his personal achievement, which makes him, like John Soane, an architect's architect*, his sensitivity to the singular potential of existential phenomena in building. It is this which not only made him a forerunner of the Expressionist approach on the one hand and the Constructivist on the other but confirms above all his personal artistic stature as a master architect.

His real historical achievement was to break out of the *cul-de-sac* of nationalism to complete a fundamental reappraisal of the nature of architecture in the light of building technique, and to recognise that a non-historical, tectonic-based architecture could arise out of an examination of the how and the why of building.

It is this which equates his work in intention with the pioneering artists of twentieth-century painting, sculpture and music and elevates him to the status of a pioneer of the Modern Movement. With the building of the Glasgow School of Art the Modern Movement in architecture may be said to have begun.

*The crypts of the Soane Museum and the Library of the School of Art are the two most powerful spatial experiences in British architecture.

31

MACKINTOSH'S SCOTTISH ANTECEDENTS

David M. Walker

It is true that the Glasgow School of Art was not publicised as one would have expected it to be in the building journals of the time. But I do not think it is right to assume that it did not have an influence beyond Glasgow, where it certainly profoundly affected James Salmon and his partner John Gaff Gillespie, Harry Edward Clifford, Alan G. MacNaughtan and the group of designers associated with the firm of Wylie & Lochhead. Progressive designers will always find their way to good work which is relevant to what they themselves are seeking to achieve, irrespective of whether it is published or not. Neither George Devey nor Philip Webb allowed his work to be published, yet they were the founders of the whole Arts and Crafts movement in English architecture.

In any event, while the Glasgow School of Art may be indisputably Mackintosh's supreme achievement, arguably Windyhill and The Hill House, which were published, were historically more influential and told the other Modern Movement designers all they needed to know. Indeed, it can be argued that the significance of Mackintosh's revival and development of the Scottish roughcast vernacular tradition of the sixteenth, seventeenth and eighteenth centuries has not always been as sharply defined by the present generation of historians as it ought to have been. If you read Raymond McGrath's *Twentieth Century Houses* (1934) and really think in the context of Robert Mallet-Stevens's work about his remark to E.A. Taylor, quoted by Tom Howarth*, that if he were God he would design like Mackintosh, it seems that the significance of his work was remembered more specifically in the 1930s when the development of modern architecture was still very recent, than it is now. Whenever it was made, Mallet-Stevens's compliment was more than a very well-informed courtesy to a Scottish visitor. Even though Mackintosh could secure little or no significant architectural business after 1912, it is wrong to assume, as many tend to do now, that the death of the Glasgow Style during World War I signified that his influence was at an end. In 1934 McGrath was in no doubt that the architecture of Mackintosh's houses had had a profound effect on the most advanced domestic work of the preceding decade; only the decorative style of their interiors had gone out of fashion, and, however painfully, Mackintosh had recognised himself that this could not be developed further when he changed course into the Viennese mainstream of twentieth century decorative design in 1911.

Mackintosh was not, of course, the first to rediscover the possibilities of the Scottish roughcast vernacular, which was revived in James MacLaren and Dunn & Watson's buildings at Glenlyon in Perthshire and Lorimer's cottages at Colinton, Edinburgh, as Robert Macleod and I showed in 1968, when these predecessors were less well known than they are now. Indeed, it can be argued that the Scots roughcast tradition never quite died. William Burn must have harled his Scots Tudor Auchmacoy, Aberdeenshire, in 1831 from choice, for it was built anew and its idiom was echoed on a smaller scale in countless farmhouses and manses. David Bryce, Burn's partner and the successor to his Scottish practice, equally had no hesitation in using harl* in such houses as Keiss in Caithness on the medium scale and Cortachy in Angus on the largest. But three qualifications have to be made: Bryce's harled houses were mostly remodellings where harl was used to unify masonry of more than one build, and all were for old nobility and gentry to whom harl was a mark of ancient lineage, whereas to the bourgeoisie, after 1850, harl tended to be seen as a cover-up of inferior

*Thomas Howarth, *Charles Rennie Mackintosh and the Modern Movement*, second edition, London, 1977.

*Lime-based roughcast with local sand and pebbles riddled to an even size.

*Stugged: surface of stone hacked or picked to a regular stippled pattern. Snecked: irregular coursing, with small stones or snecks where the levels of the coursing are changed. Coursed: squared but not polished in regular courses.

building materials, stugged, snecked or coursed rubble* with polished dressings becoming the norm. Mackintosh's early work, Redclyffe at Springburn in Glasgow (1890), is a very fair example, somewhat in the mould of J.J. Burnet, of this worship of visibly solid construction in building. But although Bryce had maintained the roughcast tradition, his baronial style with deeply moulded corbel courses, cannon water spouts and generous moulded ashlar dressings, was far removed from the vernacular houses of the lesser gentry, with their simple harl and small, deeply recessed openings, sometimes with not even a margined or moulded doorpiece. When harl was revived for the smaller house

Keiss Castle, Caithness, by David Bryce, 1862.

Below: Cortachy Castle, Angus, by David Bryce, 1870. The old house on the right has been remodelled to match Bryce's new wing on the left (since demolished).

Kilneiss, Glencairn, by J.J. Burnet (1884). *Left:* rear elevation. *Above:* front.

*Cap house: with attic roof structure recessed from wall face within parapet.

Left: Studio house at 1 Belford Road, Drumsheugh Toll, Edinburgh, by George Washington Browne, 1891.

in Scotland in the 1880s and early 1890s, the handful which stand out from that time are surprisingly all English-inspired.

J.J. Burnet's Kilneiss of 1884, for the painter James Paterson, drew upon E.W. Godwin, American Shingle style and the Japanese, and W.L. Carruthers's three large houses in Inverness, Carrol and Rossal of 1888 and Lethington of 1892, leant upon the neo-Tudor of his old master, Sir Ernest George, while Thomas Leadbetter's Mell Mohr (originally Dun Dhu) of 1886 at Loch Ard is an earlier and rather less successful essay in much the same idiom. All these have sandstone dressings at the openings, the Inverness houses also having half-timbered gables like those by C.F.A. Voysey of the 1880s. At Ramsay Gardens, Edinburgh, designed by Stewart Henbest Capper for Patrick Geddes in 1892, which is also largely English Arts and Crafts with red tile roofs and just a few Scottish motifs, many of the openings are without dressings. Had it been harled as originally intended, Martin Hardie's Tudor studio house at Drumsheugh Toll, Edinburgh, designed by W. Eden Nesfield's ex-assistant, George Washington Browne, in 1891, perhaps with his old master's Plas Dinam, Montgomery, in mind, would have been even more memorable for its clean-cut contrast of roughcast solid and undressed void. Fresh and adventurous though most of these were, Burnet's and Capper's especially so, it was in the work of James MacLaren's circle that the new Scots vernacular-modern of plain, roughcast solid and unemphasised undressed void was first developed, exactly parallel with Voysey's English equivalent at Bishop's Itchington in Warwickshire, 1888. First came MacLaren's thatched cottages, basically of Devon-Dorset types, at Glenlyon, together with the farmhouse there, with its cubic main mass and cap-house* like roof structure in 1889–90. Then, in 1891, followed the remodelling of Glenlyon House by MacLaren's successors, Dunn & Robert Watson, in which the small windows pierced in the walls represent the original genre as well as the new, and the hotel, built anew, which has an absolute simplicity that recalls the style of such seventeenth-century Scottish mansions as Auchterhouse in Angus. Although Thomas MacLaren experimented

35

Auchterhouse, Angus, 17th century, altered in 18th century.

Fortingall Hotel on the Glenlyon Estate, Perthshire, by Dunn & Watson, 1891.

Below: Glenlyon House remodelled by Dunn & Watson, 1891.

Cottages at Fortingall on the Glenlyon Estate by James MacLaren, 1889-90, from *The Architect*, 10th July 1891.

Glenlyon Farm House by James MacLaren, 1889-90.

with his brother's idiom in his houses at Doune, and although Lorimer developed the Glenlyon cottage themes much further in his Colinton cottages of 1893 onwards, substituting tile and slate for MacLaren's thatch, we have no evidence that Mackintosh ever saw any of these, but at the very least he must have seen, and probably kept, the splendid plates of the Glenlyon buildings published in *The Architect* in June 1891.

It is significant that the architects of all these works, with the exception of the Beaux Arts trained Burnet and Capper, were all either London Scots or trained in London. It is, therefore, less than surprising that Mackintosh's first building in the roughcast vernacular, the now destroyed and sadly unrecorded remodelling of the Inn at Lennoxtown, Stirlingshire (1895), was, as Andrew McLaren Young pointed out in his 1968 catalogue, directly modelled on his sketch of The Rising Sun at Wareham in Dorset – even without the evidence of the sketch, the oblong openings of small paned casements would still have been unmistakably English.

The Lennoxtown Inn was, of course, only the trial run. Because of both its basically Georgian structure and the symmetry of its prototype, it was still symmetrical and its openings had dressed margins. By Windyhill in 1899 and particularly The Hill House in 1902, Mackintosh had adopted an asymmetrical manner of composition, with carefully balanced random fenestration closer to the style of the MacLaren circle but much more distinctively Scottish in proportion and profile; as in their designs at Glenlyon, all forms of window surround have been dispensed with, the buildings consisting only of simple roughcast rectangular masses punctuated by cylinder and semi-cylinder and pierced by void, with glazing which is English vernacular from his sketchbooks at what Raymond McGrath correctly described in the language of the 'thirties as the sunrooms of the ground floor and Scottish mid Georgian at the sashed windows above. If one discounts the roof structure of The Hill House and chimney above it, superbly composed though they are, and really studies the elevations of The Hill House, particularly the cubic mass of the dining room arm of the south front with its carefully balanced asymmetrical voids of upright and horizontal rectangles, something very close indeed to the cubic house of Mallet-Stevens and his followers can be seen. It is not hard to see why Mallet-Stevens said what he did or why McGrath discounted Mackintosh's decorative art as 'details, signs of the *Art Nouveau* and in no way representative of his serious art' and praised him with C.R. Ashbee, Voysey and George Walton as 'one of those who had done much of our hard work for us'. In his simple but brilliant geometrical masses of roughcast punctuated by unadorned openings, the vertical windows balanced against the unmullioned oblongs of the large-windowed 'sunrooms' in seemingly random arrangement, it can be claimed that Mackintosh had come closer to the so-called 'white' modern domestic architecture of the late 1920s and 1930s than any of the others. Only MacLaren's farmhouse comes near to having the same qualities; although I would not underrate Lorimer's cottage houses at Colinton, which were outstandingly successful of their kind. The warm, small-scale, cosy charm of red-tiled jerkin head roofs and stone-silled windows were far removed from the infinitely bolder, large scale masses of Windyhill and The Hill House, their austere sculptural qualities subtly emphasised by the narrow colour range of grey harled walls and grey-blue slate. It would be overstating the case to suggest that the cubist domestic style of the 1920s and 1930s would not have developed exactly as it did without Mackintosh: unquestionably it would since its roots were less stylistic than functional and structural – even if many of its products were brick rather than concrete. Nevertheless, I think it can fairly be said that Mackintosh was in the very forefront of those who anticipated and helped create that style in the years before 1914.

Colinton Cottage, 23 Pentland Avenue, Edinburgh, by Sir Robert Lorimer, 1893.

CHARLES RENNIE MACKINTOSH: THE INTERNAL REALITY OF BUILDINGS

Thomas Howarth

Among the most difficult aspects of the design process that must be mastered by the architectural student are those of spatial organisation, a sense of scale, and the paramount importance of human values. It has been rightly said that the plan is the generator of a building; that, indeed, is where design begins. However, it is the three-dimensional interpretation of the plan, the concept of spatial relationships and the exploitation of light and shade that in the hands of the master give vitality to a project, introduce a sense of magic and, with careful detailing, transform building into architecture, and construction into art.

The psychological impact of the modulation of interior spaces is dependent upon appropriate changes in level, in width, height and depth of successive volumes, and the relationship of these one to another; they are, in fact, the basic elements in the architect's aesthetic repertoire. It is the quality and character of internal spaces defined by the use of colour, texture and pattern and supplemented by furnishings and works of art that, I would suggest, constitute what Frank Lloyd Wright described as 'the internal reality of buildings' and give meaning to the external, protective shell we often describe as architecture.

In Charles Rennie Mackintosh's day, the students' design skills were developed through the study of historical examples and observation of physical phenomena, and by working with established firms of good reputation who were usually building in the fashionable classical and medieval stylistic modes or in variations on them. This kind of practical training was supplemented by evening classes in sketching, composition, building construction, and measured drawing.

During his apprenticeship, Mackintosh had a distinguished record as a student at the Glasgow School of Art and in 1891 won the Alexander Thomson Travelling Scholarship which enabled him to spend several months in Italy. This was one of his most valuable experiences. He recorded in his diary that on seeing the Palazzo Ducale in Venice, 'I was transported beyond myself and the custodian thought me distracted.' His sensitivity to the emotional effects of light is vividly portrayed in a short description of twilight in Venice – 'which bats and owls love not better than I do.' He speaks of the long shadows, increased dimensions, and enlargement of detail by shadow which this time of day produces. These observations were reflected in many of his sketches – and the lessons learned were applied later in all his architectural projects. There can be little doubt also that the contrast between life in the grey, northern, industrial city of Glasgow and the extrovert vitality of Italian cities made a deep impression on the young architect. It may be that the whiteness and elegance of the living spaces he was to create later were inspired by the memory of spiritual freedom engendered by the white, flower-decked walls of Italy – and it was to the Mediterranean world that he returned to paint towards the end of his life.

Mackintosh developed to an extraordinary degree his command of all aspects of design, from graphics through the crafts to furniture and building itself. He permitted the inner reality of his projects to unfold in a gentle and subtle manner. For example, in the broad, dignified treatment of the north façade of the Glasgow School of Art, with its richly expressive ironwork and sculptured entrance elements, the doorway itself is small and the approach restricted by a flight of steps between inwardly curved walls.

Glasgow School of Art (1896 and 1897-99). *Left to right:* entrance, vestibule, main stair, exhibition gallery.

The in-and-out swinging doors are almost of domestic proportions and one enters into a very small white-painted vestibule, so small in fact that the unobservant visitor may push through the second set of doors without noting the panelling on the left with its geometrical arrangement of square glazed openings, and the enquiry hatch into the former general office; obviously one was expected to pause here! Even the most unobservant, however, should not fail to notice the three small heart-shaped openings in the inner door frame, which are filled with brilliant blue glass. These are Mackintosh's first gestures of initiation, a tiny humane and romantic indication that the architect of this building at least recognises that familiar symbolic motifs help in maintaining human values and a sense of scale; they also stimulate curiosity and heighten the layman's interest.

Beyond the inner doors lies the main entrance hall with its arched ceiling. It is shadowy; a little borrowed light enters above the vestibule, but the observer is drawn irresistibly towards the main stairway directly ahead, which is flooded with light from a large glazed roof. The stairway is a *tour de force*, a sculptural element of great significance in the heart of the building. In its spatial qualities and structural sensitivity, it anticipates the library in the West Wing, designed and built a decade later. On the staircase, Mackintosh used overlapping planes of open, square balustrading reminiscent of C.F.A. Voysey's work; a few of the tapered, square newel posts were carried to heights of eight or even twenty-five feet above floor level. At one point, a pair of beams was projected from the gallery floor to hold the highest newel post in an affectionate embrace, a structural detail common in Japanese work and used repeatedly to support the gallery in the School library. And in the centre well there is a remarkable interpretation of Glasgow's coat-of-arms in wrought iron, rods woven like a bird's nest into the form of a highly conventionalised tree: the bird was there, as were a stylised salmon and bell – the city's emblems. I use the past tense advisedly, because the original bird and the bell disappeared long ago, just as did all the bells from the two similar metal symbols on the roof.

The heart-shaped motif from the front door appears again on the staircase and is repeated high above on the king-post of the roof truss supporting the glazed roof over the staircase well. Thus the eye of the observer is drawn inexorably forward and then upwards by the combination of increasing light intensity, the stroboscopic effect of overlapping planes of balustrading, the tall newel posts which lead naturally to the square, tapered pillars of the exhibition gallery above; and the powerful roof-truss shaped like a crossbow pointing to heaven. A *tour de force* indeed!

I taught at the School of Art in the 1940s and found it an endless source of delight. There was always something new to be discovered, or an unfamiliar experience to be enjoyed. The versatility of the architect and his inexhaustible inventiveness were astonishing. He rarely repeated himself and even in the simple patterns of nine square tiles used sparingly to decorate staircase walls, he changed the arrangement to produce hardly noticeable, subtle variations.

Small leaded-glass openings in doors provided an attractive field for varied decorative treatment, often appearing jewel-like in a dark corridor. There is always a special bonus in work of this kind; leaded glass changes dramatically in character according to the light source – a panel lit from behind is quite different from one lit from the front. The design of the lead cames and the pattern of solder, which usually appears silver, assume special significance when lit from one side; the quality of the glass, its striations, thicknesses, and the bubbles that may appear as random patterns, will emerge more dramatically if lit from the other. To enjoy the full aesthetic pleasure of such work, one should take the time to view the glass from both sides and in different lights – cupboard doors should be opened so that the glass can be seen from the inside against a window or artificial light. The cupboards in the headmaster's room at the School are excellent examples, and the effect of the glazed wardrobe doors in the white bedroom at The Hill House is quite surprising when seen against the daylight.

One could write at great length about the visual delights of the School of Art and the architect's grasp of the essential functional qualities of such a building. The partially double-banked corridor system with the great studios on the north side was ideally suited to the difficult site. An artist normally requires diffused light approximating in quality to the open air, and north light is admirable.

In the upper studios, 26 feet high, there were, in addition to the great windows, roof lights some eight feet wide parallel to the external wall, thus providing a virtually ideal working environment for the students that has rarely if ever been equalled in an art school. The studios were separated from each other by a wall suspended from the ceiling to about seven feet from the floor. Below this was a movable wooden partition, so that the whole floor area could be opened up when required. It is a matter of conjecture whether or not these partitions have ever been removed or whether, as is not unusual in such situations, flexibility became an uneconomic luxury and by common consent the movable component became a fixture.

The school project was won in competition in 1896 by Honeyman & Keppie, although every informed person in Glasgow knew that the design was conceived by Mackintosh with the support of Francis Newbery, the Headmaster. Mackintosh was only 28 years of age and a junior member of the firm and his name appeared neither on the drawings, nor in public announcements.

The architects' estimated cost of the entire building, including gas lighting, was £22,753, or £110 more if electricity were substituted for gas – an astonishingly low price even by modern standards.

Because of financial stringency the Board of Governors decided to build in two sections, the first to cost not more than £14,000; they insisted repeatedly that they needed only 'a plain building'! The tender price for the first, the eastern section, including the entrance hall and the main staircase, was £13,922.3s.8d. However, because of Mackintosh's insistence upon changes as work proceeded, the final accounts were greatly in excess of this sum. Ten years were to elapse before the Board was in a financial position to finish the building. It was fortunate indeed that circumstances delayed completion, because Mackintosh now had time to redesign the library which, in the original drawings, appeared as a somewhat mundane apartment.

Between 1897, when the first section was finished, and 1906 when approval was given for work to begin on the West Wing, Mackintosh had built Queen's Cross Church, Windyhill, a large part of the Ingram Street Tea Rooms, The Willow and Scotland Street School. He had married Margaret Macdonald in 1900 and with her had exhibited at the Vienna Secession, also in 1900, and they had been royally welcomed by their Austrian colleagues; they had shown furniture at the International Exhibition of Decorative Art in Turin (1902) where Mackintosh's extraordinary design for the *Haus eines Kunstfreundes* competition had been exhibited. It has been said that in Europe at this time he was the best known and one of the most highly regarded of the avant-garde architects then practising. He had become a partner with Honeyman & Keppie in 1904, and his future seemed secure.

**Haus eines
Kunstfreundes**

Several of Mackintosh's projects represented his own (and his wife's) convictions unimpeded by the wishes of a client and are therefore important to this paper; three must suffice – the *Haus eines Kunstfreundes* competition design of 1901, the Mains Street flat, and No. 78 Southpark Avenue.

Mackintosh's approach to design is, perhaps, best exemplified by the account written by Mr W. W. Blackie of the evolution of The Hill House project. Mackintosh insisted on spending some time with the Blackie family before putting pencil to paper 'to judge what manner of folk he was to cater for.' There is nothing unusual about this way of working; it is an arrangement that might be made by any competent architect. Agreement was quickly reached on materials, general architectural character and other matters; it was confirmed by a subsequent visit to Windyhill (1899-1901), which Mackintosh had designed for W. R. Davidson. Mr Blackie goes on to say, 'Before long he submitted his first designs for our new house, *the inside only*' (my italics). 'Not until we had decided on the inside arrangements did he submit drawings of the elevation (*sic*). The first design was not approved. Therefore, in a very few days, he sent us a new set of drawings which were accepted . . .' It is regrettable that the original sketches do not survive. It would have been instructive to have seen the changes made to meet the client's wishes. However there must have been agreement on all fundamentals, because The Hill House stands as one of Mackintosh's major achievements and Mr Blackie, who speaks enthusiastically of their association, was persuaded to include the superb wrought iron gates and other items he had eliminated earlier on grounds of cost.

In the case of the *Haus eines Kunstfreundes*, the competition conditions were the only constraints imposed upon the architects and they emphasised the necessity for generous public rooms befitting the home of a connoisseur of the arts who would entertain lavishly.

Apart from a few features reminiscent of Windyhill – notably a small courtyard and pool, and the tightly planned vestibules – this design is quite unlike any other: here he was free to do as he wished, and this project enables us to assess his progress fairly. He was competing against, among others, M.H. Baillie Scott, one of the leading architects associated with the English Arts and Crafts movement and a very popular figure in Germany. It is interesting to note that in his beautifully illustrated book *Houses and Gardens* (1906) Baillie Scott says – 'It appears to be a growing custom with the principal furniture firms in Germany to invite representative architects to contribute . . . it has been Mr Mackintosh and myself who have represented the British section.' He

Haus eines Kunstfreundes, 1901. Model made by students of the Glasgow School of Architecture and Manchester University for the Mackintosh Exhibition, Edinburgh Festival, 1953, designed by T. Howarth and the late Robert Hurd. Four models were made and given afterwards to the Glasgow School of Art.

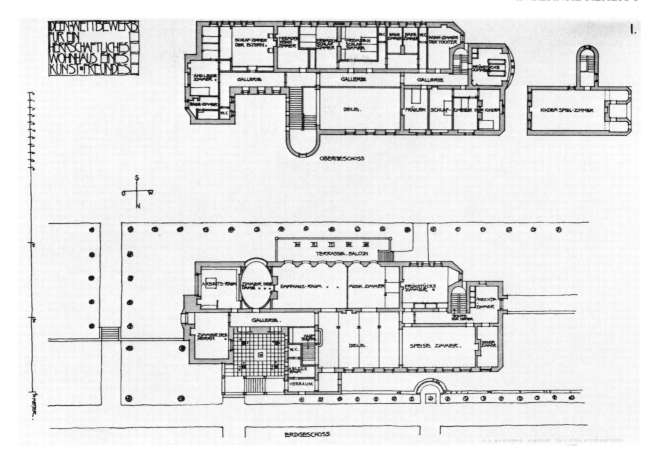

Haus eines Kunstfreundes, 1901. Plans from *Meister der Innen Kunst*, published by Alexander Koch, Stuttgart.

adds that Germany has set an example which might well be followed in Britain 'where, so far, furniture is still considered a commercial product merely, and its design as hardly worthy of serious study as an art.' These observations serve to emphasise the difference between the Continental European and British attitudes to design.

Mackintosh orchestrated the spaces in his project with great care and masterly precision. The tiny vestibules opened dramatically into a two-storeyed, galleried hall (32 ft × 22 ft). Details of the gallery were developed from Queen's Cross Church, and the design of the pendants clearly anticipated the School of Art library. The dining room (30 ft × 17 ft) opened directly off the hall, from which it was separated by a movable screen; the reception room and music room, designed *en suite* and also separated by a movable screen, connected with the hall by wide double doors.

In accordance with British and European custom in large houses, a special room was provided for ladies and another for gentlemen, to which they might withdraw independently for conversation. In those happy days, it was recognised that the sexes indeed were different and that there was merit in providing an opportunity for social exchange for each group – for a short time at least – during the course of an evening. Mackintosh's ladies' room was an elegant oval, his favourite feminine symbol; his men's room, a more prosaic rectangle, was isolated at the end of a corridor. Incidentally, there were no washrooms provided for the convenience of guests, so presumably the fine staircase to the upper floor would be heavily used on special occasions.

The hall and dining room, the reception and music rooms, which together represented about fifty per cent of the total ground floor area of the house, combined to form a magnificent space for entertaining, thus meeting the principal requirement of the competition. The music room with its remarkable organ case and the *en suite* reception room were white, with a row of tall, elegant

43

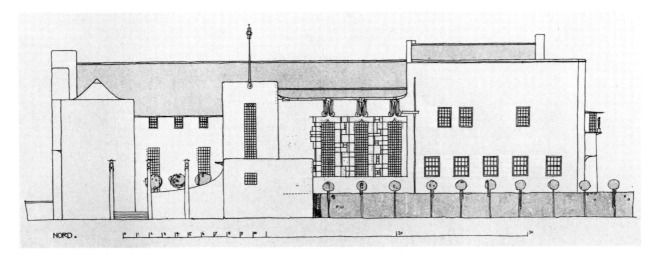

NORD.

Haus eines Kunstfreundes, 1901.
North elevation.

bay windows on the south wall all opening on to a raised terrace overlooking the garden – an ideal arrangement of formal entertaining. Artificial lighting was provided by rows of groups of four lanterns, exactly like the Mains Street examples without the saucer-like caps. Each bay was to have a pair of tall panels of female figures either stencilled or embroidered – certainly designed – by Margaret, and the organ case was flanked by a larger pair to match. This suite was to be a brilliantly rich, scintillating composition.

Thus Mackintosh played on a wide range of emotions, each room being considered not as an independent compartment in the traditional Victorian manner, but as an integral part of a carefully modulated overall spatial concept with, no doubt, the assumed advantages of European domestic central heating. The upper floor was planned with a fine parents' suite to the east and the nursery wing well separated from it by guest rooms. The only incongruity seems to have been the placing of the WCs. Each was isolated on an outside wall at the end of a narrow corridor, a peculiarly Victorian response that must have amused the more sophisticated Europeans. A children's playroom was designed in the roof space with access by a separate stair to a breakfast room on the floor below, which was served by food lifts from the main kitchen. The elegant bay window in this room combined with the two deep bays and tiny balcony in the playroom to produce externally a richly modelled effect worthy of Le Corbusier.

I have illustrated the children's room rather than the well-known public rooms to demonstrate Mackintosh's concern for detail even in smaller and less conspicuous places. In the centre of the floor was a square carpet with a tapered column at each corner rising to the arched ceiling. The columns represented trees and each carried a conical wire framework, a convention representing branches in miniature, on which were 'leaves', probably electric lightbulbs, since there is no evidence of light fixtures elsewhere. The columns may have been intended to suggest a fairy 'ring', a feature popular with the romantics of the day. The illustrator Jessie M. King, a friend of the Mackintoshes, cultivated a fairy ring of poplar trees in her garden which she showed me with great pride in the 1940s – an unforgettable meeting.

We can only speculate as to whether or not the Mackintoshes intended this to be a square 'ring', but the trees did modulate the space of the room and provide a transparent effect of enclosure that children would have enjoyed. They were also offered intriguing alternatives: two deep bays, with bench-like seats, that gave access to the tiny balcony; a larger bay window with built-in seats and a refectory-type table; and in the centre of the west end of the room, a fine Mackintosh fireplace with a high guard rail – this was obviously the cosy corner for winter days. The room was panelled to the springing line of the ceiling and, of course, was decorated with patterns of squares, rose motifs and a few hearts. Rather like the white drawing room at The Hill House (designed a year later), the children's room, therefore, was carefully arranged – 'zoned', in modern parlance – for at least four distinct uses and was large enough for other activities of different kinds. The floor is carpeted, but no chairs are shown. The *pièce de résistance* was a panel over the fireplace by Margaret Mackintosh, obviously the awakening of Sleeping Beauty, a typically sensuous design that complements the fairy ring.

The powerful sexual overtones in Margaret's craftwork and painting, and especially in that of her sister Frances, are not only obvious, but seem to be unique among women artists at the turn of the century; they deserve closer analysis than is possible here. Whether we accept Mackintosh's claim that 'Margaret has genius,' or P. Morton Shand's condemnation that she was one of the main stumbling blocks in his career, it would be difficult to imagine Mackintosh's domestic interiors without her contribution. We shall never know whether or not Margaret had more than a superficial influence upon the strictly architectural aspects of his work – conceptual planning, spatial organisation, massing, choice of materials and so forth – although it would seem most unlikely. But there can be little doubt that Mackintosh, the completely dedicated architect, respected his wife's contribution and was happy to have her collaboration. The homogeneity of their interiors depended entirely upon the harmonious integration of the work of both architect and artist, and this was seldom in doubt.

But we must return to the *Haus eines Kunstfreundes*. The rectilinear form of Mackintosh's project, with its central spine wall, permitted simple roof-lines, massing and fenestration which he used to express the inner reality of the building. Hermann Muthesius, author of *Das englische Haus*, claimed with some justification that 'the exterior architecture of the building exhibits an original character unlike anything else known. In it we shall not find any of the conventional forms of architecture, to which the artist so far as his present intentions

Haus eines Kunstfreundes, 1901. Childrens' Room.

were concerned was quite indifferent.' Although its appearance would have been unfamiliar to Europeans at the turn of the century, the *Haus eines Kunstfreundes*, in mass and fenestration, was essentially Scottish in character.

The competition came at a crucial point in Mackintosh's career, and we can recognise its influence on The Hill House (1902-04), the Willow Tea Rooms (1903-04) and the Library of the Glasgow School of Art (1906 and 1907-09), three of his most important contributions. Although he never had the opportunity of building a house on such a grand a scale, there can be no doubt that his Viennese friend Josef Hoffmann used it as a model for his Palais Stoclet, Brussels (1905), the most complete and splendid example of the Secessionist style still extant in Europe.

120 Mains Street

The interiors that Mackintosh and his wife designed in 1900 for their first home confirm without doubt their concept of the ideal living environment – in general terms, drawing rooms and bedrooms would be white, hallways and the environment for the serious ritual of dining would be dark. All furniture, furnishings, and light fittings would be specially designed to harmonise with the setting, or in certain cases be duplicated from other projects where economy, or aesthetic considerations demanded.

All rooms were sparsely furnished and positively bare by contemporary standards, with plain floors, walls and ceilings. But they were astonishing in their unity, harmony of parts, and striking originality. They constitute a very important chapter in the history of interior design: it is instructive to compare them with Baillie Scott's work of the same date at Blackwell in the Lake District.

Several good photographs of the Mains Street flat were reproduced without comment in a special issue of *The Studio* in 1901, but no other journal seems to have been interested. It was left to E.B. Kalas, a visiting French critic, to interpret the Mackintoshes' achievement – but for a French audience – in 1905.

Kalas was enchanted by their exquisite taste and masterly handling of space, light, and colour. He especially eulogised the 'virginal beauty' of their white rooms which provided a unique escape from the dirt and grime of the industrial city, and the fashionable clutter of the middle-class Victorian house. In his opinion, the Mackintoshes were 'two visionary souls in ecstatic communion – wafted – aloft – to the heavenly regions of creation . . .'

In observing the furniture and the decorative aspects of these interiors, it is easy to overlook Mackintosh's skilful control of natural and artificial light. In the Mains Street drawing room he used tightly stretched, white muslin window curtains, which are excellent diffusers of strong daylight. In front of these he hung rectilinear panels of the same material with simple patterns embroidered by Margaret, probably in the delicate greens and purples they favoured. These were suspended from a deep picture-rail, or plate-rail that was taken right round the room as an optical device to reduce the lofty proportions to a more acceptable scale.

The artificial lighting was originally by gas, with the customary central ceiling fixture, which Mackintosh removed. He covered the outlet with a large, white-painted, square panel from behind which narrow gas pipes were extended, given an elegant twist and carried to the four corners of the room to supply groups of four suspended lighting fixtures. Photographs taken at the time show only three of the four groups in place, but Mackintosh would not have left such a careful arrangement incomplete, and no doubt the fourth group was added after the picture was taken. There were, therefore, to be sixteen individual lamps, and the gas supply to each group of lamps was controlled by pulling on long cords, a rather primitive system to achieve the effect that with electricity would have been provided by dimmer switches.

Most of Mackintosh's fixtures were designed for electric lighting and by modern standards of illumination would be considered inadequate. Moreover, recent research has shown that the carbon filament bulbs then in use were only of 25 or 50 watts. As usual Mackintosh seems to have been somewhat ambivalent in his approach and the aesthetic often took precedence over the practical. He favoured an enclosed shade from which light was directed downward, while

Mains Street Apartment, 1900.
Drawing Room.

the room was softly illuminated by reflected light, enriched by the subtle jewel-like blues and purples of coloured glass inserts. Sometimes gas-lights, as at Windyhill and The Hill House, were enclosed in large, box-like lanterns with opaque glass sides open at the bottom.

The white drawing-room was some eighteen feet square and about twelve feet high. Mackintosh installed a magnificent white panelled fireplace with a mantelpiece 7ft 3in. long. The sensuous curve of the horizontal fascia to the top shelf is characteristic, and is repeated many times as a vertical motif in Margaret's stencilled and appliqué designs, where it is usually adapted to represent a human figure.

The miscellaneous pieces of furniture, arranged almost at random it would seem by the photographer, included a fine double bookcase with splendid leaded-glass door panels and a central magazine rack. There was also a well-designed writing desk with characteristic repoussé metal panels by Margaret that are identical in style with a panel she designed in 1896, now in my personal collection.

These outstanding pieces were accompanied by three chairs with very high (5ft 3in.) backs and a low arm-chair in dark oak, replicas of those used at the Argyle Street Tea Rooms. There was also a small white table with a wide top that gives it an appearance of instability, and a large heavy wing chair in dark oak. All these pieces are in the Hunterian Art Gallery at the University of Glasgow, as indeed is all the other important furniture from the dining room, bedroom and study.

The Mains Street flat was seen by some perceptive individuals as an oasis in a cultural desert. To others, the chairs looked uncomfortable and the setting

78 Southpark Avenue, 1906.
Dining Room, as reconstructed
in the Hunterian Art Gallery,
University of Glasgow, 1981.

seemed so carefully ordered as to discourage the cosiness and niceties of normal family life. It would be interesting to speculate as to whether these interiors would have been very different if the Mackintoshes had had children. We must remember, however, that dress, deportment, manners and way of life in Britain at the turn of the century were very different from ours today; there can be no doubt that Mackintosh's chairs were graced by people who knew how to use them. And his beds were quite luxurious!

Chairs

The most controversial pieces of furniture designed by Mackintosh were undoubtedly chairs, which he used as a means of expressing his dissatisfaction with the existing order of things. As Mackintosh's friend and colleague Herbert MacNair explained to me as we walked in the Argyllshire countryside, they used to place tracing paper over illustrations of fashionable pieces of the day and experiment with new forms that were usually remote from the original model. Backs would be extended, arms splayed, rails deepened and modelled, stencilled fabric, mother-of-pearl or ivory inlay introduced and so forth. For his own apartment at Mains Street, Mackintosh designed a heavy, box-like wing chair, thinly upholstered, which provided excellent protection from the draughts that bedevil dwellings in Great Britain. I have sat in this chair on several occasions when visiting the Davidsons at 78 Southpark Avenue and can vouch for its protective qualities — and its relative immobility. It seemed to wrap around one like a wooden cloak and isolate one from the rest of the room.

Mackintosh's high-backed chairs with an oval top-rail are conventionalised tree forms, symbols expressive of the upward, surging vitality of so much of his work. One of the models has a pierced, crescent-shaped, flying bird motif; the other — and there are only two kinds with oval top-rails — has a more subtle element, a removable heart-shaped panel which could be covered with a coloured or stencilled fabric to add interest to the composition. These chairs can stand alone, or in pairs as sculptural elements as, for example, in Fumihiko Maki's

Robie House, Chicago, 1908. Dining Room. Architect: Frank Lloyd Wright. Note the curious lamps attached to each corner post of the table – an extraordinarily impractical detail.

Detail of Dining Room Chair, 1897, by Mackintosh. This detail of the back of the oval top-rail of a tall dining chair should be compared with those shown on p.48 which have the flying bird motif. Comparison with Wright's Robie House dining chairs demonstrates the contrasting styles of the two architects.

Austrian Embassy in Tokyo, or be placed around a refectory-type dining table as the architect intended at Mains Street, and 78 Southpark Avenue.

The introduction of the excessively high back, 53in. or more from the floor, with its obvious disadvantage of imbalance, seems to have been a feature employed only by Mackintosh and Frank Lloyd Wright. Mackintosh's first chairs with the oval top-rail appeared at the Argyle Street Tea Rooms in 1897. The tall ladder-backs have 18th-century farmhouse antecedents and were of a kind favoured by the Shakers in America. Those with the oval top-rail were very light and much more refined, with elegantly formed frames, tapering from a rectangular section at floor level to an attenuated cylindrical section at the top. The oval top-rail was of aerofoil form, beautifully modelled and threaded through the frame.

As I have observed elsewhere, the high-backed chairs grouped round a dining table may create a remarkable sense of intimacy, of enclosure, in fact a room within a room. We can only assume that Mackintosh recognised and intended to achieve this effect. The surviving picture of his own dining room at Mains Street shows only two high-backed chairs, one at either end of the refectory-type table – a very formal arrangement indeed. My recollection of dining with the Davidsons at 78 Southpark Avenue in the 1940s is of low-backed chairs which provided a much more informal setting – the high backs were placed against the wall.

Mackintosh, however, was not alone in developing high-backed dining chairs; Voysey used more modest, traditional ones at his own house, The Orchard, in 1900, and Frank Lloyd Wright introduced high backs of more stocky proportions in the dining room of the R. Harley Bradley House, Kankakee, Illinois, also in 1900. These seem to have had a stretched fabric back below a deep rectangular top-rail. The Susan L. Dana House of 1903 in Springfield, Illinois, had much heavier dining chairs with backs made from equally-spaced vertical strips of square section which were almost identical to the Robie House examples of 1908. These are of the same height as Mackintosh's, but the sense of enclosure is emphasised.

I spent four or five days with Wright at Taliesin East, Wisconsin, in 1956, and during our discussions of the early days and of the small exhibition of Mackintosh's work and photographs that I had brought with me, he said that he did not meet the Scottish architect during his visit to England in 1910 to see C.R. Ashbee. Nor would he admit to familiarity with Mackintosh's published work, although he said he was acquainted with it through the pages of *The Studio* and German magazines.

As a visiting professor at Berkeley, California, also in 1956, I sought out Charles Greene and Bernard Maybeck, about whom we knew little because no major research on either man had been published. Both were getting on in years and communication was not easy, but I examined most of the buildings in the Bay area designed by them. The work of the Greene brothers, firmly set in the Arts and Crafts tradition, was of especial interest for its unusual detailing, superb craftsmanship and lively response to climatic conditions. Neither Charles Greene nor Bernard Maybeck was able to contribute anything of significance to the Mackintosh story, although Maybeck, when shown a picture of The Hill House library said disdainfully, '*this* isn't a fireplace' and drew for me an unintelligible spider's web of lines which he said *was* a fireplace.

In considering the two crucial figures of Wright and Mackintosh, the sequence of events is interesting if one wishes to determine who anticipated whom. The first illustrations of Mackintosh's high-backed chairs appeared in *The Studio's* special number, *Modern British Domestic Architecture and Decoration* (1901), where the Mains Street interiors were shown. It would seem, therefore, that Wright had experimented with a high back certainly as early as 1900, but the characteristic heavy dining chair of the Dana and Robie houses appeared after *The Studio* publication in 1901. Such questions are really only of academic interest, but one can assume that in this case at least, Wright was a follower rather than an originator – unless, of course, they both arrived independently at similar conclusions by using common precedents.

In general, Wright's early domestic interiors have a sophisticated, cosy, earthiness – and I have examined many of them throughout the United States – that is quite unlike the refined austerity and meticulous sensitivity to detail that characterises the Scotsman's work. We must remember, too, that Mackintosh's most remarkable achievements were concentrated in a distressingly short professional career of little more than ten years, from 1896 to 1906, whereas Wright's brilliant prodigality extended over three professional lifetimes. He

Detail of Writing Desk, 1903, by Mackintosh. This exquisite black-lacquered writing desk, made of mahogany enriched with mother-of-pearl, ivory, and leaded enamelled metal, is, in my opinion, the finest piece of furniture Mackintosh designed. A somewhat inferior copy was made for his own use and is in the University of Glasgow collection.

I have chosen this photograph with its reflections and shadows to emphasise the mysterious, spatial qualities of this fascinating piece. There are letter-racks on either side of the deep central section. The racks are of two different depths, the shallow ones concealing 'secret' compartments that are accessible by removing the back.

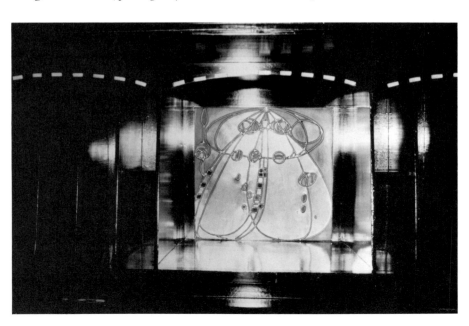

'Blackwell', Lake District, 1900. Architect: H. Baillie Scott. *Right:* Drawing Room Fireplace and Ingle. *Below:* detail of firedog. The mountain ash inspired the decoration of this house, and in the white drawing room the fireplace and built-in seats are flanked by slender columns with beautifully carved capitals of tree form. Originally this room was sparsely furnished in the Sheraton style and none of the pieces was designed by Baillie Scott. The plastered ceiling and deep frieze were decorated with plant and flower motifs in low relief; there was a large rug on the floor and the ingle and window seats were covered with frilly chintz. A heavy electric chandelier hung from the centre of the ceiling. When I visited the house in 1982, it was completely unfurnished and the drawing room had much of the scale and quality of the drawing room at 78 Southpark Avenue, except that the details throughout were in the best English Arts and Crafts tradition, exemplified here by a detail of one of the firedogs in wrought iron decorated with brilliantly coloured enamel flowers and berries.

78 Southpark Avenue

was born in 1867, a year before Mackintosh, and continued working until shortly before his death in 1959: Mackintosh died in 1928, thirty years before Wright.

The significance of the Mains Street flat may easily be overlooked by designers in the 1980s who now take for granted the revolutionary principles introduced by the Mackintoshes. Light, airy and sparsely furnished rooms with carefully designed everyday things, including textiles and works of art for every part of the house, became increasingly fashionable in Europe during the 'thirties, 'forties and 'fifties as Bauhaus ideals were widely disseminated and modern Scandinavian influence penetrated the West.

Like William Morris and his Arts and Crafts followers in England – and Frank Lloyd Wright in the U.S.A. – Mackintosh was deeply concerned by the poor design quality of everyday things. When he made his first visit to Vienna with Margaret in 1900 and exhibited there, he was delighted to find many kindred spirits. He, Josef Hoffmann and other members of the Secession shared common objectives and became firm friends. Hoffmann visited the Mackintoshes in Glasgow and Fritz Wärndorfer followed in 1902 – both, therefore, would have seen the first section of the School of Art and other work in the city. Unquestionably they would have been entertained at the Mains Street flat. Hoffmann, with the financial backing of his banker colleague Wärndorfer, for whom Mackintosh was to design the music salon in Vienna, established the Wiener Werkstätte in 1902. At this time, Mackintosh was invited to go to Vienna and set up a studio and metal workshop. This tempting offer, which he turned down, was a measure of the high regard in which he was held in Continental Europe. Had such an invitation come a decade later he would, no doubt, have accepted, but in the meantime even the Secession itself had disintegrated.

The Mackintoshes moved from Mains Street to 6 Florentine Terrace, Glasgow (renamed 78 Southpark Avenue) in 1906. Their new home was the end unit of a stolid, undistinguished terrace of Victorian houses. Mackintosh gave it a new door, opened several windows in the gable wall and transformed the interior.

All the furniture, fireplaces and light fixtures were taken from Mains Street to the new house, and similar colour schemes used. Desmond Chapman-Huston, a close friend of the Mackintoshes, stayed with them from time to time, occupying the small, unique guest quarters made out of an attic in the roof '. . . with a little flower-filled balcony'. He described the house as 'a unity, perfect

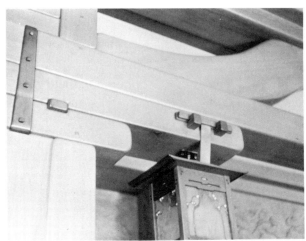

Above: Charles Greene at his studio in Carmel, California, 1956, with one of his chairs.
Right: The Gamble House, Pasadena, California (1908). Fireplace detail.
Architects: Greene and Greene. Note the superb detailing, rounded angles, polished steel strapwork, and the lantern with decorative leaded glass panels. The woodwork and detailing is quite unlike that of either Wright or Mackintosh.

from top to bottom'. Lady Alix Egerton of Bridgewater House, a much-travelled mutual friend, maintained that the attic was 'the loveliest lodging in the world'.

Sadly, the Mackintoshes only enjoyed the Southpark Avenue house for seven years; in 1913, they left Glasgow and moved to England. The house remained unoccupied until it was purchased in 1918 by W.R. Davidson for whom Mackintosh had designed Windyhill at Kilmalcolm in 1899. All the furniture from Windyhill would not go into the Southpark Avenue house, and a number of the larger pieces, including a fine white bedroom suite, lighting fixtures, and an enormous T-shaped oak bookcase, were stored in a basement room at the Glasgow School of Art where I came upon them, neglected and virtually forgotten, in the early 1940s. They were placed on public display by the late Sir Harry Barnes and myself, when, in 1947, we converted the former Board Room into a Mackintosh Room. The light fixtures and the bookcase are still there, and the other pieces are exhibited elsewhere in the School.

I met the Davidsons first in the Autumn of 1940 when I was preparing material for my first lecture on Mackintosh, delivered to the Provand's Lordship Society, Glasgow, in March 1941; we became good friends, and my wife and I frequently visited 78 Southpark Avenue. Our most memorable visit was on the evening of 13th March 1941: after dinner we left early and, as we walked to the gate, we heard the unmistakable sound of a pathfinder aircraft. When we neared our apartment half an hour later, we could hear the explosions and see the spectacular defensive pyrotechnics of the first devastating air raid on Clydeside. Shortly afterwards, my favourite 'Greek' Thomson church at Queen's Park, a few minutes walk from home, was completely destroyed by incendiary bombs.

These experiences prompted me to discuss with Mr Davidson the future security of the Mackintosh objects in his possession. As a trustee of the Mackintosh estate, he had taken care of the residue of property, furniture, drawings, etc. – then considered practically worthless – that were left after Margaret's death and the Mackintosh Memorial Exhibition of 1933 which he arranged in Glasgow.

Through the good offices of two senior professors whom I knew well – Professors Fordyce and Walton – I urged the University to try to acquire 78 Southpark Avenue in order to preserve it and its contents, if ever it came on the market.

Mr Davidson, a staunch devotee of the Mackintoshes whom during the course of my research I always found to be well-informed, kindly and patient, died in 1945. The University was successful in negotiating the acquisition of the house in 1946, and the Davidson family bequeathed the Mackintosh collection of furniture and drawings to the University in memory of their father.

In December 1946, I published two illustrated papers, one for the *RIBA Journal*, 'A Mackintosh House in Glasgow', and the other for the *Architectural*

Review, 'Some Mackintosh Furniture Preserved', which, naturally, drew world-wide attention to the commendable action of Glasgow University, and to the generous Davidson Bequest.

Incredible as it may seem now, another twenty years were to elapse before the contributions of the Glasgow designers, and of Mackintosh in particular, were to receive the recognition they deserved in academic and professional circles, and among the general public.

World War II ended in Europe in 1945 and at that time it was economically impossible for the University to turn the house into a museum. It was therefore used as a staff residence and for some years was occupied by Professor John Walton and his family.

In the early 1960s, the University proposed to demolish the whole terrace to make room for the new Hunterian Art Gallery, and despite many protests, did so in 1963. But, mercifully, the late Professor Andrew MacLaren Young of the History of Art Department had arranged for a careful record to be made of the interiors and for the removal and storage of all the original panelling, fixtures and fittings, with the objective of reconstruction when the new Hunterian was built.

One cannot give enough praise to Glasgow University, its administrators, and the dedicated staff who ensured the safe keeping of these somewhat fragile

Glasgow School of Art. Library, 1906 and 1907-09. The interior reality exemplified.

Glasgow School of Art: Exterior of Library Wing. The external expression of the interior reality.

and certainly vulnerable artefacts and who with the help of the architects William Whitfield of London virtually recreated in fact and in spirit the Mackintosh interiors of 1906. It was a thrilling experience for me to watch the unfolding of this project; here, to the great credit of all concerned in this faithful reconstruction, visitors from all over the world may recapture something of the magic, of the inner reality, of the Mackintoshes' own home.

The sequence of events in this latter stage of the Mackintosh story is of particular interest and demonstrates the difficulties of safeguarding our cultural heritage in times of change and economic stringency.

Perhaps some more personal references will be forgiven, for in this context they seem important. My book, the result of some eight years of research, was published with considerable difficulty in 1952. The publishers claimed that the subject – *Charles Rennie Mackintosh and the Modern Movement* – was so highly specialised that the first edition would take at least ten years to sell out. They were right: the second edition did not appear until 1977 – twenty five years later.

In the meantime, Robert Hurd and I designed the first Mackintosh Exhibition for the Edinburgh Festival of 1953; it subsequently toured schools of architecture in England before being shown at the R.I.B.A. in London and finally arriving at Glasgow City Art Gallery in Kelvingrove. Fifteen years later, Andrew McLaren Young, then Richmond Professor of Fine Art at the University of Glasgow, staged the magnificent memorial exhibition of 1968, the centennial of Mackintosh's birth, again for the Edinburgh Festival, and produced a superb catalogue. The exhibition went on to the Victoria & Albert Museum, London, and to Vienna. At this point, Robert Macleod published his important book drawing attention to the influence of Mackintosh's contemporaries on his work and philosophy, and Harry Barnes published a well-illustrated monograph on the furniture in the Glasgow School of Art collection.

We persuaded the Corporation of the City of Glasgow to acquire the Ingram Street Tea Rooms in 1950, and although the Tea Rooms were subsequently closed, leased and eventually demolished, the interiors and contents were recorded and stored by the City for reassembly, originally for use in a future extension of the Glasgow School of Art; they are now part of Glasgow Museums' collection. With the elegant reconstruction of the Southpark Avenue interiors in the Hunterian Art Gallery, which were opened in 1982, and the Willow Tea Rooms as models, public support for a future Ingram Street reconstruction should not be difficult to obtain if, indeed, such a project were considered desirable.

In 1971, T. Campbell Lawson, who had purchased The Hill House in 1952, offered it for sale, together with its furnishings, to any organisation prepared to ensure its preservation. In the following year, the Royal Incorporation of Architects in Scotland raised a guarantee fund for its purchase and established a trust to maintain it as a house with lettable space, rather than as a museum. Its importance as a national monument was recognised in 1982, when the National Trust for Scotland assumed responsibility for its maintenance and preservation as a museum open to the public.

Despite the efforts of scholars and others seeking to establish Mackintosh's place in history – and the foregoing is but an outline of events over the past forty years – it was in fact the sale of a single chair that, through the activities of the commercial world, made Mackintosh a household name.

In 1973 Sotheby's auctioned a chair from Miss Cranston's home, Hous'hill, Nitshill, Glasgow. It was purchased by an American collector for £9,300, and the subsequent publicity focused the attention of dealers and collectors everywhere on an unsuspected and lucrative market – almost overnight Mackintosh became news. Also in 1973, an Italian firm began to reproduce carefully documented Mackintosh furniture in the Hunterian Museum and Glasgow School of Art collections, and the Charles Rennie Mackintosh Society was founded with Patricia Douglas as Honorary Secretary.

In 1979 Sotheby's sold Mackintosh's writing desk to the University of Glasgow for £89,000, then claimed by the press to be the largest sum ever paid for a piece of twentieth-century furniture at auction. Roger Billcliffe published his splendid and meticulously researched *catalogue raisonné* of Mackintosh's furniture, and Christies sold a small, white oval table for £30,000 in the following year. The first major overseas transaction came in 1983-84, when, to preserve part of Canada's cultural heritage, the Federal Government of Canada stopped a sale in Monaco of five pieces of Mackintosh furniture that Sotheby's had discovered in Vancouver and which had, to all intents and purposes, disappeared over fifty years before. The five pieces acquired by the Royal Ontario Museum, Toronto, consisted of a single bed, washstand, dressing table and mirror from Miss Cranston's White Bedroom at Hous'hill, and a white cabinet, similar to those in the Southpark Avenue drawing room. The negotiated purchase price was about $602,000 (more than £300,000).

During the past decade we have seen the publication of a spate of books and articles on the Glasgow designers, the proliferation of Mackintosh 'souvenirs' and bric-à-brac of all kinds – and the manufacture of 'in-the-style-of' furniture. There is obviously a danger of Mackintosh becoming a cult figure as his name and work are exploited by the commercial world, but little can be done to prevent this.

On the other hand, an attempt is being made by responsible people in Italy, Spain and Canada to make genuine reproductions available to the public. The pioneer in this field, Filippo Alison, an architect and professor at the University of Naples, published in 1974 a very well-illustrated monograph in English on Mackintosh as a designer of chairs. Alison is a design consultant with a major Italian firm whose reproductions have been distributed throughout the world. Roger Billcliffe is design consultant to the Spanish firm, and we can therefore be sure that its products are of good quality and faithful to the originals. I serve in a similar capacity with a Toronto-based company that has an Austrian craftsman-president who is a devoted admirer of Mackintosh.

Since original pieces are few and far between, and in any case prices are far too high for the average purchaser, there seems to be a genuine need for reproductions of quality that can be enjoyed by a wider public. All such work, however, should bear the maker's imprint to prevent deception when in the future a reproduction might be mistaken for an original.

As we have noted, Mackintosh made a profound impression on the emerging Modern Movement in Austria during the early 1900s but, for personal

Sketch for a Glass Skyscraper, 1920. Architect: Ludwig Mies van der Rohe.

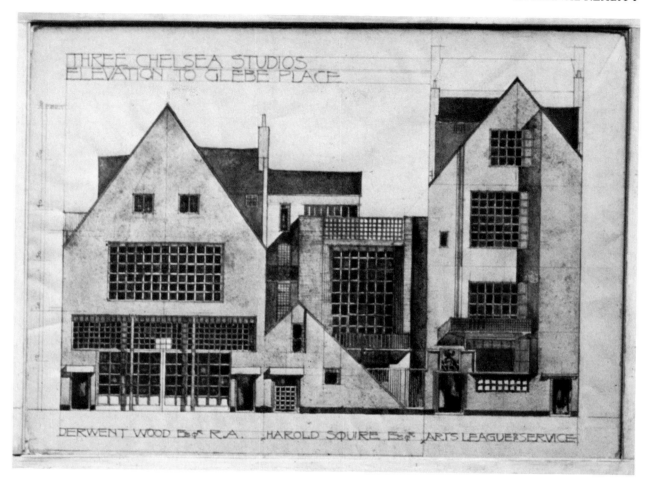

THREE CHELSEA STUDIOS
ELEVATION TO GLEBE PLACE

DERWENT WOOD Esq. R.A.   HAROLD SQUIRE Esq.   ARTS LEAGUE SERVICE

Studio Residences, Chelsea,
London (1920). Architect:
Charles Rennie Mackintosh.

reasons, he was unable to sustain this initial impetus. There was also a serious schism in the ranks of the Secession, and Fritz Wärndorfer, who had been Hoffmann's principal supporter, emigrated to America in 1913, the year in which the Mackintoshes left Glasgow. The outbreak of World War I in 1914 dramatically interrupted cultural exchange at an international level, and the influence of the Glasgow Style, the Secession and Art Nouveau was therefore short-lived and did not in any real sense survive the war.

The 1920s saw the emergence of new philosophies, new materials, new building techniques, industrial design, and a new style known now as Art Deco, evidence of which can be recognised in the Mackintoshes' work for Bassett-Lowke and in their fabric designs.

To throw into sharp focus two of the main and divergent streams of architectural design at that time I have selected two illustrations of unrealised projects designed in the year 1920: the first, Mies van der Rohe's glass skyscraper, a truly remarkable – and some would say ominous – harbinger of the shape of things to come; the second, Mackintosh's romantic concept of studio residences in Chelsea, London. Seen from the perspective of the 1980s, in a society that has grown tired of impersonal buildings, especially tall ones, and with the recent emergence of a new style – post-modernism – in which familiar traditional elements are combined with modern materials and dramatic colour arrangements, there can be little doubt that in terms of visual character, the public and many professionals would prefer the Chelsea project to Mies's glass skyscraper. It may well be that in the future we shall see the merging of these streams and the creation of a more humane environment in which the internal reality of buildings in Mackintosh's terms, and the external expression of that reality, will be fully realised.

EDGAR WOOD AND MACKINTOSH

John H.G. Archer

Few architects have been associated directly with Charles Rennie Mackintosh. However, there are unmistakable signs of correspondence between him and Edgar Wood (1860-1935), who stands to Manchester as Mackintosh does to Glasgow.* Similarities between the two men have been detected by several writers who have seen associations stronger than the general ones born of the 1930s, when *The Architectural Review* invoked the spirit of Walt Whitman and

*For additional information on Wood, *see* J.H.G. Archer, 'Edgar Wood: a Notable Manchester Architect', *Trans. of the Lancs. and Cheshire Antiquarian Society*, vols. 73-74, 1963-64, pp.152-187, which includes a *catalogue raisonné* of Wood's works; J.H.G. Archer, 'Edgar Wood and J.H. Sellers: a Decade of Partnership and Experiment', in Alastair Service (ed.), *Edwardian Architecture and its Origins*, 1975; Michael Bunney, 'Edgar Wood', *Moderne Bauformen*, vol. 6, 1907, pp.49-76; T. Raffles Davison, 'Edgar Wood – Architect', *Architecture*, vol. 2, 1897, pp.99-112; Manchester City Art Galleries, *Partnership in Style*, 1975 (a well-illustrated exhibition catalogue).

Lindley Clock Tower, Huddersfield.

[1] *The Architectural Review*, vol. 75, January 1934, pp.1-2.

[2] Thomas Howarth, *Charles Rennie Mackintosh and the Modern Movement*, 1952 (2nd edition 1977), pp.251-252 and plate 89.

[3] Nikolaus Pevsner, *The Buildings of England: Yorkshire, the West Riding*, 1959, p.275 and plate 70.

[4] Robert Macleod, *Style and Society*, 1971, p.114.

[5] Hermann Muthesius, *Das englische Haus*, three vols, Berlin, 1904-05. *See* vol. 1, p.171. (I am indebted to Mr John Mitchell for the translation.) For an abbreviated English edition in one volume, *see* Dennis Sharp (ed.), The English House, 1979.

[6] It has now been secularised and renamed the Edgar Wood Centre.

[7] Edgar Wood's father, Thomas Broadbent Wood, is cited in S. Peter Bell, *Victorian Lancashire*, 1974, pp.105-106. For a study of contemporary Nonconformity *see* Clyde Binfield, *So Down to Prayers*, 1977.

[8] For Barlow's patronage *see* Elizabeth Conran, 'Art Collections', in J.H.G. Archer (ed.), *Art and Architecture in Victorian Manchester*, 1985, pp.65-80.

[9] The fullest contemporary record of Wood's work to be published appeared in *Moderne Bauformen*, vol. 6, 1907, pp.49-76. His work was first noticed in the German press in *Dekorative Kunst*, vol. 2, 1898.

gathered them within the memorable and now historic category of 'pioneers'.[1] Thomas Howarth, whose notable book first placed Mackintosh within national and international contexts, illustrated some of Wood's principal works and listed him among those with whom Mackintosh shares 'the spirit of secession'.[2] Nikolaus Pevsner, too, perceived 'connexions with Mackintosh and Glasgow' when he encountered one of Wood's more widely known works, the clock tower at Lindley, Huddersfield, of 1899-1902.[3] More recently, Robert Macleod linked the two men as 'great provincials' and exponents of the 'so-called Art Nouveau' in the chapter on 'The Moderns' in his *Style and Society*.[4] However, all of these were preceded by a distinguished contemporary, Hermann Muthesius (1861-1927), who appears to have judged Wood's position most perceptively. In *Das englische Haus* (1904-05), he contrasts Wood with 'the large majority of the London Arts and Crafts people in whose work sobriety predominates' and describes him as a link between England and the 'poetic fantastic north of Britain in which the popular Celtic element is most evident', which could have meant only Mackintosh and the work of the Four.[5]

Of the instances cited, only Pevsner's comment makes stylistic connections, which is appropriate because, although the observation shows Pevsner's characteristic acuteness, there is relatively little close stylistic correspondence between Wood and Mackintosh, and it is through the interpretation of dissimilar works that their likenesses emerge.

The provincial worlds of Wood and Mackintosh were very different. Mackintosh belongs firmly to Glasgow, whereas Wood's practice was only nominally Mancunian. The city provided him with his formal training and a professional base for thirty years, but he built nothing in its centre and only one major work, the First Church of Christ, Scientist (1903-08), within its boundary.[6] Wood's true province was the Pennine borderland between the twin regions of south-east Lancashire and the West Riding of Yorkshire. It corresponded with his family and social background, which represented a union of the two: the Woods were from Lancashire and owed their prosperity to banking and cotton, while his mother's family, the Sykeses of Lindley, near Huddersfield, served the woollen trade. Both belonged to the Victorian industrial gentry and were active in civic affairs and public life. The Woods, in particular, provide an excellent illustration of the radical, Nonconformist, Liberal, entrepreneurial tradition, and this distinctive background was important to Wood's outlook and career.[7]

The major area of his patronage approximates to a triangle formed by Manchester, Rochdale and Huddersfield. Within this, a heavy concentration occurs about a smaller triangle between Middleton, his home town, Rochdale and Oldham. These three are central in the crescent of textile towns that curves across the Pennine foothills to the north of Manchester. Then still physically separate, such towns were highly independent. Provincial to Manchester, they enjoyed a life and culture whose richness has largely escaped social historians' attention. The Manchester Royal Exchange was the hub of their financial world, but *The Manchester Guardian*, the Hallé Orchestra and a taste for literature that encompassed a revival of dialect prose and poetry nourished intellectual and imaginative qualities that are often overlooked in accounts of contemporary northern life. The appreciation of the visual arts was not ignored. It was, for instance, a near neighbour of the Woods, Samuel Barlow (1825-93), a bleacher of Stakehill, whose independent judgement in the 1870s made him one of the earliest collectors of Degas and Pissarro, and Wood's architectural independence and imaginative fancifulness were only possible through a benign patronage that was as important to him as was Fra Newbery's or Miss Cranston's to Mackintosh.[8] Many of his larger commissions were from within the circle of his family and their friends. Their outlook was cultivated, independent and far from insular. Their trade was international, and they will not have regarded it as exceptional that illustrations of their houses and churches were published abroad.[9]

Despite Wood's increasingly wide reputation, his native town remained the most fruitful source of his commissions. He repaid Middleton with a vision of life as it might be and a wide range of designs for a multitude of purposes. Banks, churches, memorials, schools, shops, houses and cottages were among these, but he also undertook the thankless chores of minor improvements and extensions as well as answering calls for special needs and occasions, designing anything from a cricket pavilion to an address to be presented to some long-serving citizen. *Par excellence* he was the town's architect, but his vision of an artistically and architecturally ideal environment did not save this historically picturesque little town from gradually choking as it expanded, and, ironically, the prosperity that gave Wood his opportunities led to further cotton mills and their attendant rows of terraced houses. Wood's mode of practice cannot have given an easy living: like Mackintosh he had to reconcile his ideas with professional commitments and a contractual system that was impervious to his ideals and values. Also, some clients laid down exact stipulations on expenditure.

An inspired commitment to the practice of architecture as an art appears to have stemmed from Wood's early life. His wish had been to become a fine artist, but parental prudence intervened and, after a disastrous and rebellious start in cotton, as an agreed compromise he was articled to James Murgatroyd (1830-95), the work of whose large Mancunian commercial practice of Mills & Murgatroyd included the rebuilding of Manchester's Exchange. In 1885, Wood qualified by passing the newly instituted professional examination and immediately set up in practice in Middleton. Soon afterwards, at Oldham, he opened a second office that gave him convenient access to Yorkshire, and by the early 1890s he had established himself in Manchester.

Unimpressed by his experience of a large office, Wood gradually shed formal professional conventions, adopted knickerbockers and tweeds instead of morning dress, and responded to his original vocation by practising architecture as an individual artist. G.A.E. Schwabe, who in 1893 became his only pupil and then stayed on as assistant until 1910, recalled as an illustration of Wood's attitudes that the first task he was set was to draw a bowl of roses.[1] The practice was busy, and its procedures were simple and direct. Wood designed and supervised everything personally, concentrating his energies on commissions he could handle individually. Until he was fifty, he was financially entirely dependent on his profession, but he undoubtedly benefited from his social position and from his professional status as a qualified architect. Drawing, painting and sketching were his habitual means of expression, and he adroitly turned his pictorial skills to professional advantage, presenting his designs in drawings which were often exhibited and published.[2] He made his *début* in *The British Architect* in 1888 and from 1895 exhibited regularly at the Royal Academy.[3] Several illustrations in *Academy Architecture* reveal his masterly use of line in the fashionable black-and-white style of the period, but he also used colour in a highly imaginative and experimental way in both his drawings and his architecture.[4]

The careers of Wood and Mackintosh developed through broadly similar phases, but, as Wood was eight years the senior, some aspects of his early experience illuminate Mackintosh's subsequent development. It is of less consequence that Wood remained architecturally active longer – he continued designing until his death in 1935 – because his later work does not extend beyond a stage common to each that had begun approximately thirty years earlier.

Wood's most vital years architecturally were 1885 to 1916, but from 1910, after a legacy made him financially independent, he was less concerned with the practice of architecture, and from 1922 he lived in Italy and devoted himself principally to painting and, latterly, to drawing in pastels, a medium that he used with great brilliance.[5] In Italy, he continued to take a keen interest in architectural events, including the acclaim given to the 'pioneers' in the early 1930s. His last major work, a small villa at Porto Maurizio for his own use, was shown in a fine pastel drawing exhibited at the Royal Academy in 1934.

Extremely restless and energetic mentally and physically – in the words of Schwabe, Wood was 'always hounding some new ideal'[6] – his sixty to seventy buildings confirm this in the pattern of architectural development they reveal. Their qualities are not always equal to those of the few selected to present his

[1] Schwabe, a gifted artist, was a cousin of Professor Randolph Schwabe. There were several branches of the family in Manchester.

[2] A collection of his sketches is in the British Architectural Library/RIBA Drawings Collection.

[3] *The British Architect*, vol. 29, p. 135; and *see* Academy Architecture from vol. 7, 1895.

[4] Examples of his use of colour may be found in the British Architectural Library/RIBA Drawings Collection.

[5] Works in various media are in the British Architectural Library/RIBA Drawings Collection, the Manchester City Art Galleries; the Whitworth Art Gallery, University of Manchester; and public galleries or libraries at Huddersfield, Middleton, Oldham and Rochdale.

[6] Personal letter, 12th April 1950 (author's collection).

[1] There is no published biography of Wilson, but he is the subject of several studies listed by Ian Allan in his 'Henry Wilson's Brithdir Letters', Parts One and Two, *Journal of the Merioneth Historical and Record Society*, vol. 8, no. 3, 1979, pp.277-302, and no. 4,1980, pp.409-443. For an account of Wilson and one of his major works, *see* Nicholas Taylor, 'Byzantium in Brighton', *The Architectural Review*, vol. 139, 1966, pp.274-77. This is reprinted in Service, 1975.

[2] *See* T. Raffles Davison, 1897, p.100. For Burges, *see* J. Mordaunt Crook, *William Burges and the High Victorian Dream*, 1981. For Godwin, *see* Dudley Harbron, *The Conscious Stone*, 1949 and RIBA, *Catalogue of the Drawings Collection*, 'G – K', 1973. For Sedding, *see* J.P. Cooper, assisted by H. Wilson, *The Architectural Review*, vol. 2, 1897, reprinted in Service, 1975, pp.258-279.

[3] For Shaw, *see* Andrew Saint, *Richard Norman Shaw*, 1976. For Waterhouse and Manchester Town Hall, *see* J.H.G. Archer, 'A Classic of its Age'; and for the murals, *see* Julian Treuherz, 'Ford Madox Brown and the Manchester Murals', both in J.H.G. Archer (ed.), *Art and Architecture in Victorian Manchester*, 1985; *see also* Colin Cunningham, *Victorian and Edwardian Town Halls*, 1981.

[4] A single number of *The Hobby Horse* was published in 1884. Regular publication commenced in 1886 (described as Volume 1, Number 1) and continued up to 1892. *See* Ian Fletcher, 'Decadence and the Little Magazines' in *Decadence and the 1890s*, 1979. For A.H. Mackmurdo (1851-1942), *see* Stuart Evans, 'The Century Guild Connection', in Archer (ed.), 1985, and Nikolaus Pevsner, *Studies in Art, Architecture and Design*, 1968, vol. 2, pp.132-139.

[5] *See* Stuart Evans, in Archer (ed.), 1985.

[6] *The British Architect*, vol. 26, 1886, pp.104-07, 114-15, 117 and 418.

works synoptically, but the standards of design and workmanship generally achieved reflect imagination, bursting creative vitality and a formidable force of character. Almost all of Wood's buildings have suffered some mutilation – some have suffered ravages almost worse than total destruction – but each contributes to the impression of dynamic progression that is conveyed by a survey of his work as a whole, and this, in addition to the qualities of the most memorable works, is significant in the consideration of Wood as an architect.

Restless energy and a hunger for architectural experience made Wood an inveterate traveller, and annually he took a long sketching trip for his main holiday. Numerous sketches and paintings indicate both the extent of his travels and architectural interests that range from French Gothic to the Baroque, and from English to Arabic vernacular architecture. He appears to have recorded architecture compulsively, but the one subject conspicuously neglected among his sketches is contemporary work, and practically the only exception is the small church of St Martin, at Marple, Cheshire, built by J.D. Sedding in 1869-70 but extended by Henry Wilson in 1895-96 and in 1909. This is recorded in a small watercolour sketch that catches the colourfulness of the decoration.

Other indications of Wood's architectural interests emerge from the collection of cuttings and photographs he made of works new and old. Most of the office collection is now lost, but from what survives it appears that his taste was catholic and that among contemporaries his favourite was Henry Wilson (1864-1934), J.D. Sedding's pupil and successor, with whom Mackintosh also has affinities.[1]

The opening phase of Wood's career is marked by a gradual architectural as well as professional emancipation, and he later allowed that William Burges (1827-81), E.W. Godwin (1833-86) and J.D. Sedding (1838-91), all leading architectural libertarians, were influences upon him.[2] There can be no doubt also that he was well aware of that arch-emancipator Norman Shaw (1831-1912) and, hardly surprisingly for a Manchester-trained architect, of Alfred Waterhouse (1830-1905), whose *chef d'oeuvre*, the Town Hall, 1867-77, was decorated from 1878-93 with the famous murals by Ford Madox Brown (1821-93), an artist admired by Wood.[3] Sedding, Godwin and Shaw were recognised influences on the rising generation and certainly affected Mackintosh, but there is another major source that was directly influential upon Wood and at least indirectly upon Mackintosh.

When Wood began to practise in 1885, the Arts and Crafts movement was emergent but not established. Some of its major principles had been broadcast from 1884 by A.H. Mackmurdo's *Century Guild Hobby Horse* and demonstrated by the Guild at major exhibitions.[4] Its declared objects were 'to render all branches of Art the sphere, no longer of the tradesman, but of the artist', and to 'restore building, decoration, glass-painting, pottery, wood-carving and metal-work to their rightful place beside painting and sculpture.' It was intended that they would 'stand in their true relation' not only to these but to 'the drama, to music, and to literature.' The Guild proclaimed the 'Unity of Art' and aimed to make it living, 'a thing of our own century, and of the people.' These aims were printed in each number of *The Hobby Horse*, a handsome quarterly produced in large quarto format with a striking and symbolic cover designed by Selwyn Image (1849-1930) and printed on white in an ink of opaque blackness. It was undoubtedly the most radical and striking contemporary art periodical. Two major exhibitions at which the Guild made conspicuous appearances were held at Liverpool and Manchester, respectively in 1886 and 1887. A special connection links Mackmurdo and the Century Guild with Manchester, but it would have been difficult for anyone keenly interested in the advancement of the visual arts who visited either exhibition to miss the significance of the Guild's display.[5] In this respect, the Liverpool exhibition was particularly important, not only immediately, because the Guild's contributions were outstanding, but because they were extensively illustrated in *The British Architect*, whose editor, T. Raffles Davison (1853-1937) had a keen eye for the most advanced contemporary work.[6]

Cope's Cabin, Century Guild.

The Guild presented its own products in a specially designed stand and was responsible also for another, commissioned by Cope's, the local tobacco manufacturers, for whom it also designed a 'smoking cabinet', a verandahed building, apparently timber-framed on a simple regular grid, where those suffering from exhibition fatigue could restore themselves with the aid of a little tobacco and a harmonious aesthetic environment. Undoubtedly these designs introduce many of the basic elements of the stylistic vocabulary developed by the young moderns of the 'nineties, and especially by the most influential of them, C.F.A. Voysey (1857-1941). Here, in fully developed form, are displayed the spare lines, the emphatic verticals contrasted with exaggeratedly flat cappings made up of attenuated classical mouldings (called 'mortar-board cappings' by Pevsner), and, most significant of all apropos of Mackintosh, the device of spatial enclosure by linear definition. This is especially evident in the interior of the smoking cabinet, where the bench seats are lightly enclosed and even the suspended lights extend the theme of the rectangular cage. It is a *tour de force* of economical, imaginative design in a remarkable and consistent language, and is a precursor of Mackintosh's great library at the Glasgow School of Art.

The influence of the Guild upon Wood became fully apparent in a church that he designed for the Unitarians of Middleton in 1892. It was supported by his family and provided his first major opportunity to create an architectural and decorative ensemble. His father donated a large stained-glass window that filled a nave gable. Wood intended that Ford Madox Brown should design this memorial to his mother, but ultimately he designed it himself, using as a motif a symbolic tree of life with migrant birds, a theme that is reminiscent of Selwyn Image's subject for the cover of *The Hobby Horse*. On the gable wall facing the congregation Wood and F.W. Jackson (1858-1918), a *plein-air* artist and prominent member of the Manchester School,★ painted an ambitious mural,

★*See* Michael Cross, *F.W. Jackson, 1859-1918*, 1979 (catalogue of an exhibition held at Rochdale Art Gallery).

Unitarian Church, Middleton.

*See the catalogues of the exhibitions held in 1888, 1889 and 1890.

*Illustrated by Saint, 1976, see plate 218, and by H.-R. Hitchcock in *Architecture, Nineteenth and Twentieth Centuries*, 1958, plate 106A.

and below this the church fittings gave expression to the innovative attenuation and abstraction seen in the Century Guild designs. The idea of bringing all the visual arts together may also have been stirred by the Guild's programme, although by then it had been adopted and publicised by the Arts and Crafts Exhibition Society,* but in any case it was intrinsic to the Gothic Revival and is self-evident in Waterhouse's Town Hall, where the famous murals were highly advanced.

The Unitarian church has a special significance in relation to Mackintosh because the general form of its interior is derived from the same source as the Queen's Cross church of 1897 – Norman Shaw's Holy Trinity, Latimer Road, Harrow, of 1887.* Its simple interior form and timber-lined wagon-roof were adopted by both men, but Mackintosh treated the cross-beams more boldly by leaving the steel sections exposed, whereas Wood followed Shaw more literally by casing them with brattishing.

Unitarian Church, Middleton.
Organ screen.

*For Voysey's association with Mackmurdo, *see* John Brandon-Jones, *C.F.A. Voysey: Architect and Designer 1857-1941*, 1978, and Nikolaus Pevsner's chapters on Mackmurdo and Voysey in *Studies in Art, Architecture and Design*, 1968, vol. 2. For the reference to Mackintosh, *see* John Betjeman, 'C.F.A. Voysey, the Architect of Individualism', *The Architectural Review*, vol. 70, 1931, p.96.

*Robert Kerr, *The Gentleman's House*, 1864, 2nd ed., 1865.

The significance of the Middleton church is that it accurately reflects leading influences upon an aspiring designer before the characteristic stylisms of the 'nineties had become established. The Century Guild was clearly one of these, but its influence upon C.F.A. Voysey was considerably more important, not only because he became the leading disseminator of the new mode, but in particular because, according to Fra Newbery, Mackintosh derived inspiration from him. The Guild is therefore relevant to Mackintosh as well as to Wood, although apparently less directly.*

The earliest group of buildings designed by Wood, produced between 1885 and 1892, were usually constructed in hard, imperishable, unyielding materials such as those adopted by Waterhouse to resist atmospheric pollution and remain self-cleansing. Occasionally, Wood made essays into what Robert Kerr calls 'the old English style' favoured by Shaw, but these were exceptions.* Middleton's setting was attractively rural, and it can be seen from Wood's sketches that he had an eye for the richly textured, colourful and highly pictur-esque vernacular buildings of the locality. He appears to have turned to these as models from 1893 to 1894. The cause is a matter of speculation, but the change is a mark of his emancipation. There are no known local precedents architecturally, but vernacular values were increasingly admired at that time through Morris and the Arts and Crafts movement. In addition, Wood was certainly familiar with the popular revival of Lancashire dialect prose and poetry that had been centred on the Rochdale area for a generation, and the possibility of providing an architectural equivalent cannot have been without its imaginative appeal to anyone of his temperament.[1]

Wood's early vernacular essays included every possible effect that an extremely rich tradition afforded, but this gaucheness was soon curbed by discrimination. His buildings are consistently true to their region in their materials, but these are often used with novel forms, and invariably they have entirely modern details. They are therefore outside the rationalist vernacular school admired by Lethaby.[2] Their combination of invention, free interpretation and truth to materials (in the regional and material senses) creates another parallel with Mackintosh, but in Scotland national and literary associations probably made the appeal of the vernacular even more compelling.

Banney Royd, at Egerton, Huddersfield (1900–01), Wood's most lavish tra-ditional house, is a notable example of the infusion of vernacular forms with modern values. Initially it appears to conform to the seventeenth-century manor house tradition of the West Riding, but closer acquaintance reveals that it is decidedly of its period, and, once entered, the flowing spaces and elaborate detail immediately convey the imaginative quality of Wood's architecture.[3] A *Manchester Guardian* critic once observed of his houses that 'A stately Nordic mother-goddess could have descended any of the staircases appropriately.'[4] At Banney Royd she would have found herself most comfortably accommodated.

From about 1900, expressionism became increasingly pronounced in Wood's designs, and it was at this time that definite stylistic similarities to Mackin-tosh's work appeared, most notably in the Lindley Clock Tower, which is

[1] Popular dialect writers include John Collier (pseud. Tim Bobbin, 1708–86), Ben Brierley (1825–96), Samuel Laycock (1826–93), and Edwin Waugh (1817–90). Wood designed a title page for a series of dialect books, and his friend F.W. Jackson provided illustrations for these and others.

[2] Clearly expressed in his *Philip Webb and his Work*, 1936, reprinted 1979. *See* Chapter 7, 'Theory of Architecture'.

[3] It is extensively illustrated by Muthesius, 1904–05, and in the English translation, ed. Dennis Sharp, 1979.

[4] 'Edgar Wood, Architect', 14th December 1935.

Announcement of Mackintosh's visit to the Northern Art Workers' Guild in the Guild's syllabus for 1901-02, and Mackintosh's signature appears in its visitors' book, now in Manchester Central Library. No subject was announced and no press reports have been traced. The 'Seemliness' lecture gives no information as to its intended audience, but the ms. (in ink on 17pp foolscap) has 'Xmas 1902' pencilled on the top page. The content is appropriate to the Manchester occasion, and, if an allowance is made for a confusion of Christmas and New Year, it may be assumed that this was the address Mackintosh delivered. The meeting was held at the Geisha Café, 23 Cross Street, which was near the Exchange.

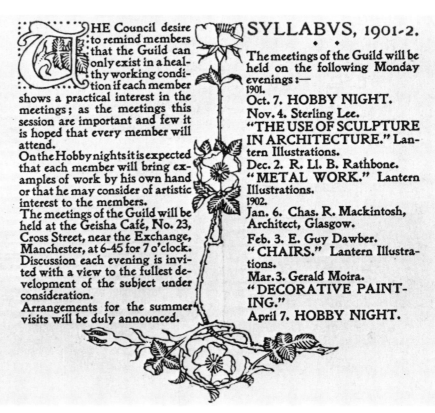

★ *See* Pevsner, 1959, p. 275.

★ *See* picture caption on page 65.

★Wood's exhibit in the 1896 exhibition, a bed, is illustrated in *The Studio*, vol. 9, 1896, p.279. In 1898, 1903 and 1911, many exhibits by him were included in exhibitions of the Northern Art Workers' Guild at Manchester. A catalogue was produced for each, and from these it can be seen that he was an extremely active and prominent member. Notices appear in *The Studio*, vol. 14, 1898, pp.284-287, and vol. 15, 1898, pp.121-127.

near Banney Royd. Nikolaus Pevsner associated it with Mackintosh because of its wilful character and exaggerated verticality. An early drawing, which shows the roof decorated with thistle motifs in wrought iron, makes the connection irrefutable.★ It is likely that the two men met at about this time, in fact on 6th January 1902 when Mackintosh visited Manchester to address the Northern Art Workers' Guild, probably on 'Seemliness'.★ Wood, a co-founder of the Guild, was its principal architect member and it is unlikely that he would have been absent on such an occasion, especially as he will then have known of Mackintosh's work for some years – in 1896 both had exhibited at the Arts and Crafts Exhibition Society in London.★

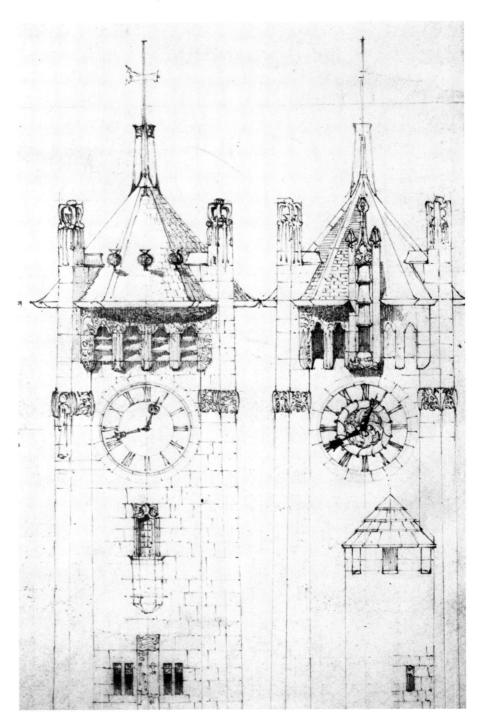

An early design for Lindley Church tower.

The First Church of Christ, Scientist, Manchester.

In terms of professional recognition, Wood was at a peak in about 1900. Three of his major buildings were produced in rapid succession: the Long Street Wesleyan Church, Middleton, 1899-1902; Banney Royd, 1900-01; and Lindley Clock Tower, 1899-1902. In 1903, he commenced his best-known work, the First Church of Christ, Scientist, Manchester, which progressed through several stages until its completion in 1908. Of necessity its design passed through a variety of drastic changes, but it emerged with a powerful coherence that relates architectural innovation and an extraordinary eclecticism. The complexity of its history is totally subsumed in the result, and the church signifies a further dramatic enlargement of imaginative expression. Nikolaus Pevsner has described it as 'pioneer work, internationally speaking, of an Expressionism halfway between Gaudí and Germany about 1920 . . .'* It would not have been out of place in Darmstadt or the Vienna Secession, and, indeed, some of its detail carries a strong hint of a Viennese connection.

*Nikolaus Pevsner, *The Buildings of England, South Lancashire*, 1969, p.48.

The First Church of Christ, Scientist, Manchester. Organ screen.

*Mackintosh's design for Liverpool Cathedral exemplifies the sculptural tendency.

*See Heinz Geretsegger and Max Peintner, *Otto Wagner 1841-1918*, Salzburg, 1964, English version, 1970. *See* plates on pp.229-231. I am grateful to Dr. Christian Witt Dörring who mentioned to me that illustrations of details of the First Church reminded him of some in the Steinhof church.

*See J.H.G. Archer, 'Edgar Wood and J. Henry Sellers: a decade of partnership and experiment' in Service (ed.), 1975.

The form of the church is its most striking feature. The plan is Y-shaped, with the arms projecting from a high, gabled nave. The main entrance is central, but a conically-capped stair turret is inserted to one side, and a generously-proportioned, machicolated brick chimney rises behind this to confirm and complete the asymmetry of the design. Vernacular character is still evident in the attractive play of traditional materials, but it is wilfully transformed by a bold licence that treats them plastically. Gables are handled as newly expressive elements by setting back the outer edges on plan to produce a canted outline above. The result on the form is dramatic. The main gable, rendered and painted white, soars high above the projecting arms, and its inclined sides, like folded wings, accentuate its height and power. The effect is completely outside the range of conventional architecture. It carries the latent sculptural expressionism of late nineteenth-century Gothic church architecture into Expressionism in the accepted sense.* The detail of the church is equally unusual in its diverse eclecticism. It draws upon the colourful vernacular of the region, the richness and variety of Arts and Crafts skills, and a new source, the vernacular of the Middle East. The organ screen, placed above the main entrance, is designed as a *mushrabiyyah*, an Arabic screen made up of rods, bobbins and small panels in a strictly geometrical pattern. Their indigenous use is in windows to admit air while providing shade and privacy, but in this instance they screened the organ without obstructing the sound. Below is a framed and panelled console screen, but the individual panels are variously patterned and modelled with circles to give abstract, asymmetrical motifs within a symmetrical whole. The screens, designed in 1908, were part of the last section of the church to be completed, which is not without significance as they show points of similarity to some in Otto Wagner's church of St Leopold am Steinhof, Vienna, 1905-07, although a definite connection between the two has not been established.* By 1907, Wood had turned away from the free-flowing lines of his previous decorative work and was becoming increasingly absorbed in rectilinear geometric patterns. He and Mackintosh were moving in the same direction, but in Mackintosh's case the influence was certainly Viennese.

A watershed occurred in Wood's career when, about 1904, he formed an informal partnership with James Henry Sellers (1861-1954), a native of Oldham who had only recently returned there after spending his working life as an itinerant assistant or 'architectural ghost', as he described himself because his designs were unacknowledged.* He was self-taught, a studious reader deeply imbued with the idea of creating a modern classicism. He attributed this to the experience of living in York, where he had found the Georgian buildings an

Upmeads, Stafford.

★ *The Architectural Review*,
vol. 91, 1942, pp.109-112.
Republished in N. Pevsner and
J.M. Richards (eds), *The Anti-
Rationalists*, 1973.

architectural revelation. In 1901 in Oldham, he had built a handsomely classical extension to the seventeenth-century house of a successful engineer, James Dronsfield. Wood's attention was drawn to this and to another house extension of 1903 for William Dronsfield. The latter was unusual because it incorporated reinforced-concrete flat-roof construction, but both were confidently modern in expression, although their classicism included some quirkiness. Introduced by an architectural photographer, the two men became associates when Wood offered Sellers space in his office to set up in independent practice. The advantages for Sellers seem obvious, but it is less clear how the arrangement benefited Wood. Sellers, as an artist and architect of character, had new ideas and experience to offer, always an attraction to a man like Wood, but it is possible also that Wood felt both isolation and the burdensome responsibilities of his position. The arrangement was successful, and the partners remained friends for life. According to Schwabe, work was discussed, but each partner remained individually responsible for his projects. Very few are in their joint names.

Soon after the arrival of Sellers, further new ideas began to appear in Wood's work. He started to adopt axial principles, classical detail and reinforced-concrete construction. After producing several houses combining flat and pitched-roof construction, in 1907 Wood built Dalnyveed, at Royston, Hertfordshire, the first of a series of flat-roofed houses that introduced a new form to contemporary domestic architecture. The best known is Upmeads, Stafford, built in 1908, which is presented in Lawrence Weaver's *Small Country Houses of To-day* (1910). Its severe, rectilinear form was considered forbidding and fortress-like – and the passing of Wood's picturesquely gabled houses was mourned elsewhere – but the descriptive account of Upmeads in the book includes an explanation of Wood's reasons for adopting the flat roof. These are notable for their rationalism and their anticipation of ideas associated with the Modern Movement of the 1930s. Hardly surprisingly, Upmeads was seen as a fore-runner of modernism by Nikolaus Pevsner, who included it in an article, 'Nine Swallows – No Summer', in 1942. ★ While in some respects this is historically justifiable, in others the house is as much at variance with Modern Movement ideology as the First Church of Christ, Scientist, is with the rationalist ethic within the Arts and Crafts movement. The divergence does not arise from the stylistic eclecticism of the house, which includes Tudorish windows and classical detailing, but from the expression Wood sought to extract from the use of the flat roof. He appreciated that it freed the plan from the limitations imposed by pitched roofs, but he exploited this to gain a sculpturally expressive external form, as is clear from the evolution of the plan in the series of houses. At

Dalnyveed the forms are strictly rectangular; at Upmeads, the main entrance is recessed in a shallow concave bay that is central in its elevation; and in the final house of the series, one that Wood built for himself in 1914–16 at Hale, Altrincham, Cheshire, the plan form is virtually Baroque – the entrance front is almost semi-circular and its flanking elevations are deeply concave. Their curves are not expressed internally, and the major rooms are made rectangular by absorbing them within the depth of the walls. The new technology, therefore, became a means of gaining greater formal expressiveness, and there was no question of displaying the technique itself as an architectural end. As in the First Church, the motive was aesthetic – the plastic expression of form.

The decoration of the Hale house provides another illustration of invention and imaginative eclecticism. The theme throughout is chevron patterning. It occurs in simple forms on the drive and garden paths, in a more intricate interlocking design in a panel of coloured tiles above the main entrance, and in equally rich complexity on the entrance and principal internal doors. It appears also on fireplaces, fittings and furniture. Much of the painting was carried out by Wood himself during the years when World War I left the office quiet. The similarity between this and Mackintosh's decoration at 78 Derngate, Northampton, is notable. It illustrates that both men had become absorbed in complex formal geometry as a basis for design, but the comparison also indicates their different attitudes to domestic interiors. Wood's do not maintain an absolute stylistic consistency. He produced a background that permitted selective variety and, in his own home, exploited this by introducing exotic pieces of furniture which he had presumably acquired on his travels. The modernity of both schemes is striking, and each presages the zig-zag motifs and colours of the post-war Art Deco.

The Hale house virtually marks the end of Wood's professional career and of his architectural development. However, his last house, a villa at Porto Maurizio, is not an anticlimax. It shows greater sobriety in planning, and its rectangular form may be attributed to the use of a pitched roof to give solar insulation. The structure has a reinforced-concrete frame, but this is not expressed and may have been adopted as a matter of constructional convenience. The roof is apparent, so that there is no attempt to obtain a cubic outline but, as in all of

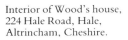

Interior of Wood's house, 224 Hale Road, Hale, Altrincham, Cheshire.

Watercolour by Edgar Wood of the villa he designed at Porto Maurizio.

*One of the mirrors is now in the collection of the Cecil Higgins Art Gallery, Bedford.

Wood's later schemes, the corners are emphasised, in this case by stencilled patterns rather than the inset quadrant modelling he had used from 1907. The main garden elevation is symmetrical and closes an elaborate formal garden in which the various spaces are divided by rectilinear open frames. The decoration, like that in the Hale house, was entirely geometrical, with gold leaf imposed on rich, subdued background colours. The general use of the chevron was carried even further, extending to mirror frames and even clothing* – unconventional colour and decoration were now added to the general unconventional rationality of Wood's dress. Despite some extravagantly Baroque features in the garden and the symphonic use of pattern and colour, Wood's last house is a quiet but rich finale to an adventurous and at times tempestuous career.

Several points of correspondence emerge from a comparison of Wood and Mackintosh. Stylistically, as has been mentioned, Wood was fleetingly indebted to Mackintosh in about 1900. This is shown in several minor ways but principally in the design of Lindley Clock Tower. It is doubtful whether Mackintosh borrowed directly from Wood, but David Walker's thorough pursuit of Mackintosh's possible sources cites a precedent by him for the use of the shallow ogival outline to complete a wall head, a feature that is prominent on the east elevation of the Glasgow School of Art.* In Wood's Williams Deacons and Manchester and Salford Bank, Middleton, of 1892, a drawing of which was published the same year in *The British Architect*,* this detail appears above the small projecting entrance block, but at that time the architectural accent of the 'eyebrow' curve was beginning to appear quite widely, and Voysey, who was far more influential than Wood, provided a more exact precedent in his design for a studio, illustrated in *The British Architect* soon after Wood's design had appeared.*

*The Architectural Review, vol. 144, 1968, pp.355-363. See p.359 and note 10.

*The British Architect, vol. 38, November 1892, p.349.

*For an earlier example, see the house by Leonard Stokes in Academy Architecture, vol. 1, 1889, p.14. For the Voysey design, see British Architect, vol. 38, December 1892, p.404. It is illustrated by Walker, The Architectural Review, vol. 144, 1968, p.360.

Such borrowings are of only minor importance in the stylistic milieu of a period when the prevailing free style depended on wide-ranging eclecticism. In the design of Lindley Clock Tower, for example, Wood's debts to Henry Wilson and J.D. Sedding probably exceeded those to Mackintosh. Wilson's design for a tower for St Mary's, Lynton, exhibited at the Royal Academy in 1892, is particularly notable for its emphatic lines of vertical expression and their dramatic arrest by a wide-spreading, swept metal roof. This in turn derives from Sedding's design for a tower for St Clement's, Bournemouth, exhibited at the Academy in the previous year.* Sedding, Shaw and Wilson, all highly influential upon both Wood and Mackintosh, were notable contributors of major and minor themes and details to the rapidly evolving contemporary vocabulary. They helped to create what Mackintosh described as a 'common book of architecture' for the period, and in time both Wood and Mackintosh enlarged this themselves.*

*See Academy Architecture, vol. 4, 1892, p. 40, and vol. 3, 1891, p. 35.

*Note overleaf.

*Lecture 'On Architecture', 1893. Mackintosh expressed his admiration for Norman Shaw, John Bentley, John Belcher, G.F. Bodley, Leonard Stokes, and J.D. Sedding. All were potent examples to the succeeding generation. Robert Macleod cites this passage and the architects in *Charles Rennie Mackintosh*, 1968, pp.37-38; 2nd edition 1983, pp.38-39.

[1] Both forms of imagery are included and discussed in John Dixon Hunt, *The Pre-Raphaelite Imagination 1848-1900*, 1968.

[2] Thomas Howarth, 1952, pp.229-233.

[3] In 1901, for instance, Wood decorated a room at Birkby Lodge, Huddersfield, with an elaborate frieze depicting scenes from the Arthurian legends. It is illustrated in Margaret Richardson, *Architects of the Arts and Crafts Movement*, 1983, and Manchester City Art Galleries, *Partnership in Style*, 1975.

[4] See *Dekorative Kunst*, vol. 7, 1901, pp.170-174, 176-178, 184, 185. An excellent cabinet of 1898-99 by Otto Wagner is illustrated in Peter Vergo, *Vienna 1900*, 1983, plate 3, and a sideboard exhibited at the Secession by Kolo Moser is illustrated in Peter Vergo, *Art in Vienna 1898-1918*, 1975, p.64.

[5] L. Hevesi, cited in Peter Vergo, 1975, pp.63-64, and Nikolaus Pevsner, *The Sources of Modern Architecture and Design*, 1968, p.142.

[6] *Dekorative Kunst*, vol. 2, pp. 273, 277.

[7] For the Secession, *see* Peter Vergo, 1975, p.67. It is possible also that Wood may have adopted the chevron from Islamic designs. He visited southern Spain, North Africa and Egypt but is not known to have travelled so far by 1907-08.

[8] Mackintosh's attitudes and ideas, particularly as presented in his lectures, are discussed by Robert Macleod, 1968.

Striking similarities between Wood and Mackintosh are seen in the parallel courses of their architectural development. They appear to have been architects of a kind. Idealistic, imaginative and highly volatile as designers, they brilliantly captured the aesthetic transition from nineteenth-century romanticism to the more abstract forms of twentieth-century design. In the first half of their careers they may be seen as late successors to such major romantic visionaries as William Burges and Pugin. Muthesius was correct in pointing to the poetic element that links Wood with his Scottish contemporaries. It is seen most clearly in the decorative detail of the sculptural chimneypieces, naturalistic carving and painted friezes of his interiors and is closer to the mainstream of Pre-Raphaelite art than is Mackintosh's weird figurative imagery, but however divergent the latter may be in mood and expression from Wood's, it has the same ultimate origin.[1] Thomas Howarth lucidly discusses Mackintosh's sources and relates them to the Scottish renaissance of the 1890s,[2] but the less involved symbolism in Wood's imagery is more overtly literary. Neither of the two architects, of course, could have succeeded in creating such imaginative worlds had their symbolism not been considered appropriate by their respective patrons.[3]

Extraordinary creative energy later led each man, early in the twentieth century, to a profound transformation in personal style. Apparently impelled to adopt formal, rectilinear geometry and totally abstract decoration, each discarded the vocabulary that had first brought recognition and success. In Mackintosh's case the transition can be attributed directly to his association with the Vienna Secession and, subsequently, the Wiener Werkstätte. It probably dates from 1900, the year of his great Viennese triumph, when the Secession exhibition was devoted to the applied arts and the work of leading European designers and workshops. In addition to the celebrated room for which Mackintosh and the Four were responsible, with its sparse furniture, delicately curved fittings and ethereal atmosphere, new and more rational values were represented by excellent examples of rectilinear furniture by Koloman Moser (1868-1918) and by Josef Hoffmann (1870-1956), leading members of the Secession, as well as by C.R. Ashbee (1863-1942) and the Guild and School of Handicraft, representing England.[4] Ashbee's work was much admired and an influential Viennese critic wrote ' . . . it is extraordinary how Ashbee's furniture designs stand out. As if they came from a rectangular planet . . . everything vertical, at right angles, ninety degrees,' but Hoffmann's contemporary work was abreast of Ashbee's, and Pevsner has noted that his nickname became 'Quadratl-Hoffmann' because of his preference for the right-angle.[5]

There is less direct evidence of Wood's familiarity with Vienna, but as his work appeared in German periodicals from 1898[6] it is at least probable that he knew of contemporary Austrian events through these. Almost certainly, he will also have been aware of the illustrations of, and references to, the new forms of Austrian design that were published in *The Studio* from about the turn of the century and were given extensive coverage in 1906 in a *Studio* special publication, *The Art Revival in Austria*, edited by Charles Holme. There is a hint of Vienna about the First Church, and Wood's use of the chevron as the basis of his patterns from 1908 may have the same origin. It appeared in the decoration of the Secession's fourteenth exhibition (in 1902), and Hoffmann directly anticipated Wood's use of the superimposed W in his design for the decorative logo of the Wiener Werkstätte that was used from 1903.[7] Wood's receptiveness to the ideas of Sellers is indicative of his hunger for new avenues of thought and design at this time, and it is possible that Viennese sources may be as important to him as to Mackintosh.

Two powerful and related underlying attitudes inform the careers of both men: the desire to practise architecture as an art – a mode of personal imaginative expression – and the determination to make it modern and original.[8] To each, style was a personal matter that permitted a free eclecticism as long as fresh use was made of whatever had been adopted. Both worked creatively by constantly assimilating new forms and details, but these always emerge absorbed within, or translated into, some new form of imaginative expression.

Each was an accomplished stylist and, although Mackintosh gave even more memorable expression to Sedding's memorable words on there being 'hope in honest error, none in the icy perfections of the mere stylist', it was not style as an intrinsic quality that was repudiated, but cold historicism, the perfect reproduction of the modes of the past.

Wood expressed his views on style in a short letter to *The British Architect* in response to a question on the appropriate style for Liverpool Cathedral.[1] More combative but less grammatical than Sedding's remark, his answer is enlightening: 'No style or treatment,' he asserted, 'has any advantage over another for places of worship or anything else, it is what you do with it, the word "style" is a bad word to use and never enters the mind of an artist, it is the language entirely of the antiquarian and classifier.' In claiming in this way that it is 'what you do with it,' Wood was declaring himself an aesthetic individualist and a follower of the select school that includes the artist James McNeill Whistler (1834-1903), architects such as William Eden Nesfield (1835-88) and E.W. Godwin, and, more distantly, the high aesthetes of the 1860s and 1870s, Walter Pater (1839-94), Dante Gabriel Rossetti (1828-82) and the poet Algernon Swinburne (1837-1909).[2]

Individualism, a pronounced characteristic of Victorian religious, political and economic life, is peculiarly expressed in the visual arts by Aestheticism.[3] E.W. Godwin, Whistler's architect, was the boldest architectural individualist of his day and a leading influence on the younger architects of the 1880s, and especially after his clash with the Metropolitan Board of Works over the design of Whistler's house had made him a hero of the hour.[4] He visited Manchester in November 1878 to lecture 'On some buildings I have designed' to the Manchester Architectural Association, a body largely made up of the younger members of the profession. The room was hung with his drawings, including those of Whistler's house, and his lecture proclaimed individualism in the boldest possible terms. He assured his audience that the knell of the Gothic Revival had been sounded and that, just as they saw gas being superseded by electricity, so, 'before they had time to turn round,' the current Queen Anne style would also be gone. He invited them to be independent of fashions, to study widely, 'taking what good they could from every country and every age,' without adopting any particular style. Finally, he recommended that when questioned as to the style of their work, they should reply 'It is my own'; and with this heady advice he concluded. With this intoxicating message, there was one very sobering thought. In criticising the antiquarianism and architectural inconsistency of the Victorian age, his own work included, Godwin made an unusual claim. Architecture, he said, 'must be logical or it is nothing.' It was a message of steel that went largely unheeded.[5]

There is no positive evidence of Wood's presence at the lecture, but Godwin's visit and his memorable and dynamic message will have been long remembered in the Manchester offices, and, apart from the call for stringent rationalism, he may be said to have outlined the course that both Wood and Mackintosh subsequently followed.

Individualism is inherent in Pater's *Studies in the History of the Renaissance*, published in 1873, which sets out the principal tenets of late Victorian aestheticism.[6] In its preface, Pater argues that the value of a work of art depends upon its abstract qualities and that it can be judged only by the unique individual aesthetic response it evokes. The function of the critic is to analyse this 'reducing it to its elements,' noting it 'as a chemist notes some natural element, for himself and others.'[7] Beauty, therefore, becomes relative, with 'all periods, types, schools of taste' being 'in themselves equal.'[8] Pater judged creativity to be individualistic, not collective, and to him the principal question for the study of any period was 'In whom did the stir, the genius, the sentiment of the period find itself?' Genius, he maintained, quoting William Blake, 'is always above its age.'[9]

One does not find architects or architectural periodicals quoting Pater, but the first number of *The Century Guild Hobby Horse* (1884) opens with an aesthetic manifesto by A.H. Mackmurdo, 'The Guild Flag's Unfurling', that

[1] *The British Architect*, vol. 56, 1901, p.306.

[2] *See* Elisabeth Aslin, *The Aesthetic Movement*, 1969; William Gaunt, *The Aesthetic Adventure*, 1945; Mark Girouard, *Sweetness and Light*, 1977; R.V. Johnson, *Aestheticism*, 1969; Robin Spencer, *The Aesthetic Movement*, 1972.

[3] *See The Oxford English Dictionary* for an informative range of examples.

[4] For his biography, *see* Dudley Harbron, *The Conscious Stone*, 1949.

[5] A report is in *The British Architect*, vol. 10, 1878, pp.210-212.

[6] *See* particularly the preface and conclusion.

[7] Walter Pater, *Studies in the History of the Renaissance*, 1873, p.ix.

[8] Pater, 1873, p.x.

[9] Pater, 1873, p.x.

*The Century Guild Hobby Horse, 1884, p.8.

*The Century Guild Hobby Horse, 1884, p.8.

*'A Lecture on Art', vol. 1, 1884, pp.34–70. 'On Design', vol. 2, 1887, p.117. It should be noted also that Mackmurdo and his circle in the Guild were deeply interested in Renaissance art and architecture.

*These have been covered already by Thomas Howarth and Robert Macleod.

*Lecture to the Manchester Society of Architects, 1911.

*'Seemliness' p.1. Mackintosh's lectures are in the University of Glasgow, Hunterian Museum, Mackintosh Archive.

*'Seemliness' p.6.

presents in a less rarified and considerably more assertive form the aesthetic values propounded by Pater. A strong preference is expressed for abstraction, here called 'subjective art', which is opposed to realism, that is, 'naturalistic art'.* Unlike Pater, Mackmurdo was not concerned with analysis and critical values but with justifying his position as an artist. He associated the creation of abstract art with strength of imagination because this 'implies the power of giving what is most desired by the imaginative, namely, distinct mould of moods, and that firm insistence on individual conception, which always accompanies strong self-temperament.'*

Mackmurdo's familiarity with Pater may be reasonably assumed from this article and from others in the *Hobby Horse* by his close friend Selwyn Image.* Certainly Pater's inspiration is clear in its pages, and as it addressed directly those who were restlessly seeking new values, it establishes a link between the diffuse sentiments and aspirations later expressed by individual architects and the sources of a recognised and coherent aesthetic theory.

Neither Wood nor Mackintosh presents an easy subject for architectural interpretation. Some aspects of their work relate to major Victorian sources, such as Pugin, Ruskin, and the values of the contemporary Arts and Crafts movement,* but their work combines other-worldliness with elements of wilfulness and perversity that deny reasonable explanation, and it is not satisfactory to attribute such characteristics simply to personal idiosyncrasy. Godwin's precepts, Mackmurdo's claims, and Pater's values help to illuminate the attitudes, lives and careers of both men. Wood certainly believed that artists were 'torrents of will . . . insatiable in their hunger for experience and opportunity,'* and Mackintosh, in his lecture 'Seemliness', addressed his Mancunian audience as artists and advocates of 'individuality, freedom of thought and personal expression . . .'* The vocation of the artist, he claimed, is 'the exceptional development of the imaginative faculties – especially the imagination that creates – not only the imagination that represents,' and he attributed to this power what he described as 'the hallucinating character' of an artist's work.* The emphasis laid upon this quality echoes Mackmurdo, but the more subtle relationship seen between art and fantasy points to Pater's perception of the rôle of art. An association of individualism and romantic aestheticism provides an indispensable standpoint for the understanding of both architects.

Wood and Mackintosh may be seen, therefore, as confrères, with Wood, being senior, placed slightly closer to the sources that were formative to them both, but a discussion of two such men cannot omit all qualitative comment on them as architects. Artists by temperament and vocation, they emerge primarily as men of imagination, acute sensibility and brilliant intuition. They were highly rational in many aspects of their professional work, as is borne out by their domestic planning, but their ultimate loyalties were to expressive aesthetic values. Of the two, Wood was perhaps the more adventurous in his willingness to experiment, but, despite the memorable originality and distinctiveness of his most notable buildings – and his flat-roofed houses are unique – nothing that he produced matches the sheer brilliance of Mackintosh at his best, as in the West Wing of the Glasgow School of Art, a work of marvellously controlled expressiveness which fully embodies the aesthetic attitudes and values that inspired both men.

Despite their gifts and achievements, both Wood and Mackintosh lack that large command of plan and structure that belongs to architects of absolutely the first rank, although few would dispute that Mackintosh was an artist of genius. That these architects have different qualities, and qualities of different degree, is readily apparent. This, however, is no impediment to confraternity but one of its true conditions.

Whether Mackintosh and Wood knew one another remains an open question, but if 'Seemliness' was the lecture given at Manchester the probability becomes virtually a certainty. Mackintosh began with the acknowlegement that 'I have already had the pleasure of meeting some of your distinguished members and admiring them as men and as artists both in language and in line . . .', and if that tribute excluded Wood it would be remarkable indeed.

FRANK LLOYD WRIGHT: AN AMERICAN ARCHITECT

Don Kalec

An architect, like any artist, can derive inspiration from many sources – both natural and man-made. Far and away the dominant influence on architects during the late eighteenth and early nineteenth centuries was the classical tradition of Greece and Rome. This hold was broken, only to be replaced by another equally pervasive influence – that of the Machine Age as portrayed in the International Style. Both of these traditions were worldwide and, for the most part, they ignored regional or national traditions, aspirations and character.

Frank Lloyd Wright, like Charles Rennie Mackintosh, began his architectural career just when the classical tradition in architecture was being questioned and designers were looking for other sources of inspiration. Both men drew upon their national heritage as the main wellspring for new architectural forms. Because Wright's buildings seemed to make such a break with historic American styles, the uniquely national character of his work has been overlooked. It is also hard to identify the distinctive attributes of the American character because the United States is such a recently formed amalgam of world cultures. To find these national qualities it is necessary to go back to the beginning and see how the American character was fashioned.

The first Europeans to settle in America elected to leave a familiar world, embarked on a frightening sea voyage not knowing if they would ever see land again, and disembarked in an awesome wilderness from which they had to wrest a living. This initiation meant that only certain types of people came to the New World – and lasted – despite their national differences.

The first Americans were, for the most part, young. The rapid expansion of the United States gave young people opportunities they would not have had in Europe. In the nineteenth century, the continued growth of the country meant unusual opportunities for young architects. John Root was 23 years old when he went into partnership with Daniel Burnham, Louis Sullivan was 24 when Adler and Sullivan was formed, and Frank Lloyd Wright was 26 when he opened his office.

The early settlers were adventuresome – willing to take risks, even daring or dangerous undertakings – for hadn't their very coming to America been the greatest risk of all? Wright came from that tradition of taking chances. His buildings risked new forms, new structural systems, new materials (or new ways of using old materials), new interior spaces with new connections to each other and to the exterior, new styles of furniture and decorative arts, and new site relationships. His personal life was also one of daring, and he pushed himself into situations that were highly unorthodox. 'I went out into the unknown to test faith in freedom,' he said.

Ambition has played a decisive role in the American character. 'A better life' to the colonists meant increased wealth, power or distinction. Wright's ambition was to be the greatest architect who had ever lived. That engine drove him through 72 years of architectural practice.

The American character was formed from all these attributes and from the vast and primitive landscape where sheer survival required these characteristics to be strengthened, polished and codified into American beliefs that were shared by the community no matter what were its other religious tenets. A belief in hard work was one such precept – in order to survive and extricate from the land the riches that only back-breaking effort could obtain. Wright learned how to add 'tired to tired' working as a boy on his uncle's farm – a lesson carried over into his architectural practice where some 430 buildings were completed during his architectural career, with an equal number of unbuilt projects.

Another article of faith was that in a democracy all men were created equal. There was no noble class in America. Every man had an equal opportunity and, by dint of his own effort, could rise to whatever level hard work would take him. Americans also held that by their thinking, and believing, and hard work, they could mould a new spirit – a new country. Frank Lloyd Wright believed that this new spirit of America needed a new architecture through which to express itself.

The early settlers were also anxious to get away from authority – either religious or governmental. Many of the pioneers fled westward because they never liked (or trusted) the fledgling government of the United States. Wright was at odds with authority all his life – first his mother, and his uncles; later his friends, society and the various levels of government. He believed that the sovereignty of the individual came before the dictates of society.

There are five additional American characteristics which particularly affected Wright's architecture – the idea of freedom, the love of change, optimism, inventiveness and a belief in democracy.

The Idea of Freedom

Americans have a very particular idea of freedom. The early settlers found a land that had no boundaries – they could just keep moving on and on, looking for opportunity, for riches, for the better life. The last government land wasn't given away until 1890, when America was 114 years old. By then, the concept of the endless national landscape, ripe with possibilities, was burned deeply into the American consciousness. The endless road was the American symbol of freedom. Freedom equalled movement. Opportunity was always beckoning down the endless road. This vision of freedom influenced American architecture even before Wright's birth. The tight, boxy shells of the early colonists' houses were gradually relaxed and opened up as materials became cheaper and the landscape more friendly. The interior rooms became more open to each other via wide archways. Americans anyway rarely closed their doors.

Frank Lloyd Wright grew up during an era of rapid physical growth and social change. His father was an itinerant minister and musician, and Wright had lived in six towns in four states by the time he was eleven years old, adding two more cities before he was twenty-one.

Wright saw typical American houses (mostly Queen Anne in the Midwest) as still being cramped and confining – a big box outside with little boxes

F.F. Tomek house, Riverside, Illinois, 1907. Bands of windows (light screens) open the interiors to the exterior.

Avery Coonley house,
Riverside, Illinois, 1908.
Entrance drive vista.

inside. For him, freedom meant breaking open the box to facilitate visual and
physical movement both within and from inside to outside. He first opened up
the box with long bands of continuous windows (which he called 'light
screens'), so that the vista from within was never blocked. Later, Wright used
corner windows, removing the most confining part of a room, where wall meets
wall. He also designed banks of glazed doors which opened to broad terraces outside, dissolving whole walls so that inside living and outside living became one.

Interior box-like rooms disappeared when Wright used, in place of walls, an
arrangement of piers, fireplaces, mullions, and built-in furniture to create a
series of spaces which openly interlocked with each other. Freedom of movement prevailed.

The Darwin Martin house (1904) in Buffalo, New York, was the first plan
where normal walls ceased to exist – the ultimate destruction of the box. Groups
of birch piers clustered around, loosely distinguishing the inside from the outside,
and the various spaces within. Visual freedom and movement were possible in
every direction.

Wright evoked the spirit of the endless road more directly with his long
vistas inside and outside his buildings. In the Avery Coonley house (1908) at
Riverside, Illinois, there is an inside vista which extends over 100 feet from the
dining room at one end of the house to the master bedroom at the other end.
This is exceeded only by a parallel vista on the exterior which follows the entrance drive from one side of the property to the other as it runs alongside the
house for 120 feet. At each end, the house bridges over the drive to frame the
vista of the prairie landscape beyond.

Freed from the confines of a suburban lot, Wright created his most spectacular
vista at his home, Taliesin West (1939), in the Arizona desert. An exterior
walk, the main circulation route, begins at a large desert boulder laden with
American Indian pictographs. It passes under a low-beamed pergola and around a
narrow pool before ducking under a bridge which exactly frames Black Mountain, 25 miles away across the stark Arizona desert. This ultimate open road –
representing time as well as place – begins in the past with a native American
antiquity. It then passes through the present reality of Wright's own architecture, and projects itself out across the untouched desert to the future – the
opportunities of Black Mountain, where hoards of gold nuggets are believed
to be hidden.

Love of Change

Americans do not just tolerate change, they have a love affair with it. They are always looking for something new – which is equated with something better. The rapid growth of the country, the industrial revolution, the general prosperity brought a succession of vast changes to the average family – usually changes for the better. A dark, dank sod hut gave way to a clapboard house with curtains at the glass windows –   all in one generation or less.

Wright grew up in a period when change was celebrated – for change meant a better life. He also found in his studies of nature that change was an inevitable part of life. 'The law of organic change is the only thing that mankind can know as beneficent or as actual,' he wrote in his autobiography.

In his own work, change was manifest. Within an eleven-year period Wright's style rapidly evolved from the vertical, almost Gothic, George Furbeck house in Oak Park (1897) to the long, sleek, ship-like Frederick Robie house in Chicago (1908). Even within one stylistic period, there were wide variations due to site conditions, client's needs, economic constraints, and Wright's own aversion to developing just one expression. On the same street in Oak Park within one year Wright designed the dark, solid Arthur Heurtley house (1902) and the horizontally stacked, grey-stuccoed Frank Thomas house. Despite the variations possible in the Prairie style, Wright grew tired of its vocabulary. The major breakthrough came in 1919, when he designed the Aline Barnsdall house in Los Angeles. Three successive design-elevations by Wright show the transformation from a Prairie house to this vastly different structure. It was as if every Prairie motif were inverted – low hipped roof to flat roof; wide overhangs to no overhang; horizontal bands of windows and doors to only a few vertical slot-like openings; textured surfaces of brick, boards or stucco to smooth monolithic masses.

These themes of the Barnsdall house became the more developed themes of the precast concrete block houses (1923-1924) in southern California. This in turn changed to the more flexible Usonian houses (beginning in 1936), where brick piers and chimney masses, solid board and batten walls, and ranges of glazed doors more freely opened the interior spaces to each other and to the exterior.

While the Usonian house was the norm until Wright's death in 1959, there were many houses in his later work that owed their character only to his avoidance of rules – the hovering concrete trays above a waterfall in Edgar Kaufmann's Fallingwater, the play of various sized circular rooms around an open court in the project for Ralph Jester, and the vertical, shaft-like V.C. Morris house

Below: Arthur Heurtley house, Oak Park, Illinois, 1902. A compact, solid, masonry expression of Wright's Prairie house. *Opposite:* Frank Thomas house, Oak Park, Illinois, 1902. Although designed in the same year as the Arthur Heurtley house, this was a completely different interpretation of the Prairie house.

Edgar Kaufmann house, Fallingwater, Ohiopyle, Pennsylvania, 1936. Stacked concrete trays above a waterfall – one of Wright's most unique houses.

designed for a cliff facing the Pacific Ocean. Wright was not interested in developing a style (or even a set of rules). He wrote that he was interested in the exception that proved the rule.

Even in little things Wright sought change, development, growth. Almost every time his stationery was reprinted, Wright tried a new paper stock, changed the graphic design, or modified his logo (the red square). His own houses of Oak Park, Taliesin, and Taliesin West were constantly in a state of flux. He

Ralph Jester house, project, 1938. Model of project (roofs removed) showing the circular rooms grouped around an exterior court.

saw them as charcoal sketches – to be erased and redrawn continuously. Every new opportunity was a fresh start. The white tracing paper awaiting the architect's design was an invitation to perfection – ever new.

Optimism

Change was perceived by Americans as being for the better. The early settlers had to believe in the future, in the optimistic view that by their own hands they could make a better life. Only the optimistic survived the harsh climate, the hard physical work, and the absence of a supporting social structure.

Wright's forebears were of immigrant stock and through hard work became successful farmers in Wisconsin. To have a belief in the next crop, no matter how meagre this year's harvest, was an innate part of farming. Wright learned this lesson as a young boy working on his uncle's farm, and he never seemed to falter in a belief in the future.

In the 1930s, during the great depression, when Wright was developing his designs for a low cost house, he never became discouraged or bitter because he could no longer do the intricate oak trim, the custom-made furniture or the complex art-glass windows that he had once been able to do when his clients were wealthier. It was the passing of an era – but Wright never seemed to regret it. He worked out schemes where much simpler softwood trim, furniture made on the site by the carpenters, and ornamental jigsawed window openings did the same thing, visually, as the crafted products of a bygone era.

Robert Berger house, San Anselmo, California, 1950. Ornamental wood windows fabricated on the job site replaced costly art glass in Wright's low-cost houses.

Ocatilla Desert Camp, Chandler, Arizona, 1927. Rough boards and inexpensive canvas made a unique desert environment for Wright and his staff.

Wright loved the results just as much. It was another opportunity for creativity, another direction to explore. 'Victory from the jaws of defeat' was one of Wright's favourite expressions.

In 1927, instead of following the safe course of renting temporary living and working space for his family and staff in Chandler, Arizona, Wright, with typical American optimistic faith in striking out into the unknown, built temporary structures out in the desert. Erected by his draughtsmen in about a week, Ocatilla, a camp of rough boards and white canvas, was another optimistic chance taken – to create, to build, and to live unconventionally. Although it lasted less than a year, photographs of these desert ephemera travelled to Europe, and the ideas later became the basis of Wright's western home, Taliesin West.

Near the end of his life, Frank Lloyd Wright was asked what his favourite building was. Despite a pantheon of world-class buildings to his credit – the Larkin Company, Unity Temple, Midway Gardens, the Frederick Robie house, the Imperial Hotel, Johnson's Wax Company, Fallingwater, the Guggenheim Museum – Wright simply answered, 'the next one'.

Inventiveness

Americans have a love of tools and gadgets. They are never so happy as when they can invent something – particularly if it can be made from junk around the house and can perform some practical task. The American colonists learned to fabricate their own things because imports from Europe were so expensive. The majority of Americans were farmers who lived too far from town to shop more than once a week. They learned to use tin cans and baling wire for making and fixing and inventing. So American inventions were things useful to the common people in bettering their everyday life.

The long rifle's extended barrel and rifling increased accuracy, so that the frontiersman was assured game as he pushed westward. The sewing machine, the telephone, the electric light – were inventions that changed people's lives drastically. Often the invention was a system that enabled a product to be mass produced – like Remington's rifles and Ford's automobiles. A process of building using wood members of small cross-section covered with thin wood boards (balloon framing) enabled semi-skilled workmen to erect buildings rapidly. Coupled with the machine-produced nail, standardised lumber sizes and a railroad system to deliver the lumber and nails cheaply, the balloon frame revolutionised American building in terms of speed and cost. This was just the beginning of a stream of inventions for the building industry – bath tubs, toilets, hot-water heating, stoves, refrigerators, window hardware.

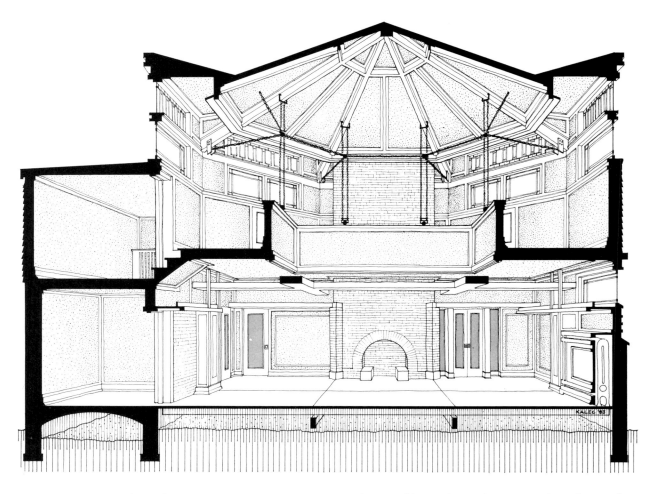

Frank Lloyd Wright Studio, Oak Park, Illinois, 1898. The horizontal chain harness resisted the thrust of the roof beams. Similar chains suspended the balcony.

Wright continued this tradition of being inventive even when the product was not a mass-produced item. In the playroom addition to his home (1895), he suspended a grand piano above a rear staircase with only the keyboard showing in the playroom. The studio addition to his home (1898) used a visible chain tension system to resist the thrust of the roof while vertical chains supported a hanging balcony.

Wright was never satisfied just to design the shell of the building. He wanted to integrate furniture, lighting, heating, and the decorative arts. Since none of these was produced exactly as he wanted it to function (or to look), Wright often had to invent new products. For his Larkin Building of 1904, Wright created the wall-hung toilet and cantilevered desk chairs to facilitate cleaning.

The electric light, a new American invention just coming into use as Wright began his career, was immediately exploited by Wright for the numerous advantages it had over gas lighting – both practical and ornamental. His own home of 1889 used electric lights above a perforated wooden grille – one of the first uses of diffused electric lighting. Unity Temple (1905), Midway Gardens (1914), and the Annunciation Greek Orthodox Church (1959) used electric lights in a rhythmic series as ornament. In his first low-cost Usonian prototype house (1936), Wright ran a sheet metal channel, with lights on the bottom and sides, down the length of the house. The feed wires were simply laid in the bottom of the channel. Easy to wire, easy to fix – Yankee ingenuity at its most basic.

For the flexibility of office sizes in the National Life Insurance Company project (1924), Wright invented modular office partitions and furniture. For the later Johnson's Wax Company (1936), Wright had to work out a whole new vocabulary of inventive products – glass tubing used for windows, skylights and partitions, metal and wooden office furniture using tubular steel supports, and round elevators with brass tube enclosures.

Wright's low-cost home designs of the 1930s were a whole system of inventions beginning with an integrally coloured concrete mat, scored with a modular unit system, poured over a gravel bed containing the heating pipes. Solid board and batten walls were placed over the scored unit lines. This was Wright's update of the balloon frame (thinner and more fire-resistant), constructed of an inner core of ¾ inch plywood with horizontal boards and battens screwed to both sides.

A feature of every low-cost, Wright-designed home was another Wright invention – the carport. He reasoned that when every enclosed square foot adds to the cost of the house, why house an automobile?

A Belief in Democracy

America was the first middle-class nation. For the first time in history the vast majority of the population were landowners and home owners. The forms of the buildings the settlers brought from Europe were vernacular rural styles – simple, unpretentious and made from natural materials, unpainted. They worked equally well in the United States, where human resources were limited. The image of these plain houses, coupled with the democratic belief that all men were created equal, fashioned communities where no man's house was too much larger or more grandiose than another's. The New England village became the symbol of a democratic architecture. Henry Thoreau wrote about the natural, unpretentious environment in *Walden*. Ministers preached and wrote extolling the moral virtues of plain living in a modest dwelling.

Frank Lloyd Wright's mother, Anna, grew up in such surroundings on a farm in Wisconsin. Her belief in the simple and the natural was reinforced by the writings of the transcendentalists – William Ellery Channing, Ralph Waldo Emerson and Thoreau. Wright remembered his boyhood home for its waxed maple floors, simple vases filled with dried leaves, good engravings framed in narrow wood bands, and simple rattan and maple furniture. This belief in the proper environment – modest, unaffected, logical – forced on the colonists by necessity, became a moral dictate, a part of Christian and democratic living. This morality was passed on to Wright through his mother.

It is no wonder that Wright reacted so strongly to the extravagances of the Victorian houses that were springing up all across the suburban prairie when he began his practice. The Queen Anne house with its gingerbread, turrets, varieties of materials, and complex floor plan was not only an aesthetic affront but a moral affront. It had nothing to do with what the reformers believed were basic American and religious values.

Cost was another anti-democratic factor. Only the well-to-do could afford a custom-designed and custom-built house. Wright believed that in a democracy every person not only had a right to a home of his own but a right to a beautiful

Herbert Jacobs house, Madison, Wisconsin, 1936. A continuous lighting fixture, made from a metal channel and standard lighting sockets, runs through the entire house.

Above: Ward Willits house, Highland Park, Illinois, 1902. The first true Prairie house – extensive and expensive. *Right:* Joseph Walser house, Chicago, Illinois, 1903. A low-cost Prairie house with all the architectural amenities.

home of his own, regardless of income. Throughout his career Wright wrestled with the problems of designing an affordable house for the average citizen. It was more important to him to solve the problem of designing a modest-cost house than to build anything else he could think of.

One of his first efforts was the Joseph Walser house (1903) for a young clerk in Chicago. Just the year before, Wright had perfected the first example of his mature Prairie house for Ward Willits, a wealthy manufacturer, in Highland Park, Illinois. The Willits house cost $20,000, which was expensive for the time. Wright democratised the Willits design to make its features affordable to average incomes – like Joseph Walser's. Sitting on a typical Chicago lot 50 feet by 150 feet, the Walser house, which cost about $4,000, had eight rooms in 2,200 square feet compared to the Willits's 1.3 acre site, 14 rooms and over 6,000 square feet. Despite its smaller size, the Walser house had all of the amenities of the larger and more expensive Willits house – low hipped roofs, art glass windows, spacious rooms, outdoor porches, a fireplace in the living room and master bedroom, changes in level, wood banding on the walls and ceiling,

Fireproof house for $5,000, project, 1905. Architectural model of the prototype, low-cost housing scheme.

and built-in furniture. Wright had worked it out so that, for one fifth of the cost, the clerk's house had the same architectural qualities as the manufacturer's.

Wright's next low-cost housing design was a fireproof house for $5,000, developed in 1905. A simple cube of concrete (for economy construction) contained a logical and direct arrangement of spaces inside – including a 15 × 30 foot living room, two fireplaces, four bedrooms and a terrace. While never constructed in concrete, this scheme became the basis for many low-cost houses by Wright and a model for other architects designing economical houses. Wright also worked on designs for multi-family housing – trying to bring beauty to those who could only afford to rent. However, Wright's larger houses have gained the world's attention, tending to obscure his efforts throughout his career to make his designs affordable for average incomes.

From 1936 (in the depths of the Great Depression) until his death in 1959, Wright developed his Usonian houses – another scheme for moderate-cost houses. Built of brick, wood and glass, used both inside and outside for economy and beauty, these flat-roofed houses opened out to private rear gardens through banks of glazed doors. The qualities these houses radiated could not be found in more expensive conventional homes. They were designed and built for newspaper reporters, school teachers, and other clients who had an appreciation of the best in design but lacked a large income. When clients of greater means wanted houses they were quite often given Usonian houses – only larger in size. In Wright's democratic architecture, wealth only bought more square footage. The qualities of space, materials, and relationship to nature were a democratic birthright that all Americans should enjoy in their houses.

The American Landscape

While all of these American social and economic forces moulded Wright's architecture, the American landscape was also an important factor in the way his architecture developed. The American landscape is at its most unique and

Melwyn Maxwell Smith house, Bloomfield Hills, Michigan, 1946. A typical low-cost Usonian house.

exotic in places like the Rocky Mountains, Yellowstone National Park, and the Painted Desert – but Wright rarely had such spectacular sites for his architecture. The majority of sites for Wright's houses did not differ all that much from some European landscapes – quietly rolling hills with meadows and clumps of trees occasionally forming forests. In these serene surroundings of the American Midwest, Wright developed the majority of his buildings. The flatness of the prairie, devoid of any vertical element, was the determinant for his Prairie-style houses. Low hipped or flat roofs hovering close to the ground, horizontal bands of doors and windows, human-scaled flowing interior spaces, and extended horizontal lines of terraces, walls and pergolas all enabled the architecture to relate to the landscape in a new but natural way. It was the idea of the prairie that inspired Wright for, by the time he began his development of the Prairie house, the limitless prairie had already been tamed where it approached the cities – subdivided into lots with newly planted trees and bushes obscuring the view to the horizon. His Prairie houses were confined to suburban lots – not one was ever built on virgin prairie. What Wright did was to evoke the character of what that suburban lot had once been.

For one thing Wright used the whole lot for the architectural composition. He didn't just put a house in the middle of a piece of property. The Prairie houses were erected with the living and dining rooms facing south towards the warmth of the low winter sun. Where lots were narrow, this meant placing the house right on the north lot line, with the major rooms facing south, so that they had vistas across the greatest amount of lawn.

As part of treating the lot as one design, the Prairie house reached out into the landscape with various architectural devices. The most extensive were porches or connected pavilions. The hot, humid summers of the American prairie promoted outdoor living where the slightest breeze could be employed. Midwestern houses always had one or more porches. What Wright did was to extend them beyond the confines of the house out into the site, so that house and landscape interlocked. This arrangement also allowed the porches and pavilions to be clear of the house and catch the prevailing east-west winds off Lake Michigan.

Other architectural projections into the landscape included walkways, sometimes with planting areas or pools in their centres, usually connecting the house with the street. Free-standing walls of the same materials as the house extended out into the site, making every part of the lot part of the architectural composition. These walls usually terminated in piers which carried planting urns – nature became integral to the architecture at the same time as the architecture was reaching out into nature. This interweaving of man-made and natural was a

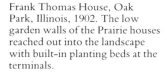

Frank Thomas House, Oak Park, Illinois, 1902. The low garden walls of the Prairie houses reached out into the landscape with built-in planting beds at the terminals.

Melwyn Maxwell Smith house, Bloomfield Hills, Michigan, 1946. Brick walls, extending from the house, turned and returned to form outdoor spaces.

principle Wright continued to use in his Usonian houses, where concrete terraces edges with broad brick steps flowed out into the lawn. Reaching out even further, low brick walls turned and turned again to form other outdoor spaces.

Away from the prairie, on hillier sites, Wright used many of the same devices to integrate architecture and nature. Garden walls circled the hilltop, connecting house and site. The plain, monolithic bases of houses designed for the prairie were extended downward to adjust the horizontal lines of the house

Frank Lloyd Wright home, Taliesin, Spring Green, Wisconsin, 1911–59. The Prairie house adapted to a steep hillside.

Frank Lloyd Wright home, Taliesin, Spring Green, Wisconsin, 1911-59. The forms of the cedar shingle roofs followed the forms of the hills beyond.

to the undulations of the hillside. Wright's own home in Wisconsin, Taliesin, was a superb example of architecture wedded to nature. The house wrapped around the hill rather than perching on top. Here, in his own house, Wright first used the local limestone, laid as it appears in natural outcroppings around the region. The use of natural materials and forms was carried ever further in the hipped roofs which had cedar-shingled forms that echoed the low hills of the Taliesin valley. Architecture and the landscape have seldom been so perfectly integrated. The site became more beautiful because of a man's intervention.

The multiformity of the landscape is particularly American. Few other countries range from the Arctic to the Tropics. Wright designed for every climate and region in the United States, and the diversity of his architecture reflects the diversity of the land. Florida Southern College in Lakeland, Florida (1938-1954) keys to a tropical environment. Built of special cast-concrete block using

Taliesin West, Frank Lloyd Wright western home, Scottsdale, Arizona, 1936. Desert masonry carries the ground form up into the architecture.

Florida, Southern College, Lakeland, Florida, 1938–54. Geometrical roof openings allow a play of light and shade in the brilliant tropical sun.

sand found on the site, the architecture is light, airy and delicate. All the buildings are linked with covered walkways for protection from the sun and frequent heavy rains. Both walls and roofs are pierced with geometric openings recalling the lacy foliage of the palm and orange trees which grow luxuriantly among the buildings.

For the walls of his desert home, Taliesin West, Wright followed the precedent of his Wisconsin house by using native materials from the site – shards of rocks, spalled from the mountains behind and found on the desert floor. Cast as facing rock in rough concrete, the mosaic-like walls looked like remains from an earlier civilisation. Ground and architecture became one. Above these ground forms, a wooden framework carried canvas panels to ward off the direct rays of the sun and provide a diffused light for the spaces below. Taliesin West recalled the pueblos and the teepees of the southwest American Indians without imitating them. 'Native architecture as she's supposed to be,' said Wright.

For the Pacific coast at Carmel, California, Wright designed a weekend cottage for Mrs Clinton Walker (1948). Sited on rocks at the ocean's edge, the octagonal living room looked out on seven sides to Carmel Bay. The native rocks continued up into the low stone walls while the stepped-out windows and blue-green roof tiles symbolised the form, rhythm and colour of the ocean.

While Wright often used materials from the site to make his buildings blend with nature, they are never 'naturalistic' like caves or log cabins. They are natural in the sense that Wright looked at the landscape – its form, structure, pattern, and growth – and then abstracted it into the architecture itself. Building and site became one, the landscape made even more intense, more beautiful because of the building. However, it is always clear what had been designed by Wright and what had been done by nature. The two are so closely bound by their similar inner character that the division doesn't matter – it is irrelevant.

People are born, grow up, are educated, work, live, dream – all in the confines of their own country. They ingest the national spirit – it is regarded as 'natural'. The truly artistic are able to integrate aspects of the national spirit in their work, condense it, codify it, and then create a work of art that is wonderfully in tune with their own time, place and purpose. Frank Lloyd Wright was such an artist. Ideas and designs from other countries certainly inspired him but, in his heart and in his art, he was truly an American architect. Walt Whitman, a favourite poet of Frank Lloyd Wright, said it best: 'When the materials are all prepared and ready, the architects will appear. I swear to you the architects shall appear without fail. I swear to you they will understand and justify you. The greatest among them shall be he who best knows you, and encloses all, and is faithful to all. He and the rest shall not forget you. They shall perceive that you are not an iota less than they. You shall be fully glorified in them.'

Mrs Clinton Walker house, Carmel, California, 1948. The forms and materials of the house are taken directly from the site.

GREENE AND GREENE

Randell L. Makinson

The impact of the Arts and Crafts movement in the United States was as varied as the topography and people of that vast country. The work of few designers, however, was as fascinating or as influential as that of the Greene brothers on the West Coast. Transforming and transcending the California bungalow, they created an architecture that was indeed both an art *and* a craft. Their care and control was complete: from landscape to book plate, no element escaped their artistic attention; striving constantly for perfection, they alone took every decision directing the superb craftmanship essential to that end, yet never alienating their skilled tradesmen, who considered it a privilege to be associated with them in their endeavour.

Charles Sumner Greene was born in Cincinnati, Ohio, in 1868 and his brother, Henry Mather Greene, under two years later, in 1870. Within a few years, the family moved to St Louis, where their accountant father decided to study medicine. Another move to Virginia followed and it was there that the brothers grew up on a farm, spending their childhood close to nature. Later, back in St Louis, their career as architects was set in motion. (Their great-grandfather had been an architect in Boston, and it seems to have been expected that they would follow the same profession.) Dr Thomas Greene enrolled his sons in the first Manual Training High School in the United States, set up by his friend Calvin Milton Woodward. Here, in classroom and workshop, the brothers not only learned and practised skills of craftsmanship but absorbed those important philosophical relationships between form and function, materials and tools. It was the knowledge and experience gained under Woodward's English-influenced manual training régime that later won for the brothers the respect and love of their workmen. Whatever they asked of their craftsmen, they themselves could do.

Henry Mather Greene and (*right*) Charles Sumner Greene, c.1890, when they had just completed their academic training and were apprenticed to major Boston architectural firms.

David B. Gamble House, Pasadena, California, 1908, archive photograph, c.1912. The broad, low-pitched overhanging roof, open sleeping porches and a clear expression of the articulated wooden structure brought to the Greene's larger bungalows an open and airy quality so appropriate to the climate and lifestyle of Southern California.

After three years, Charles graduated. A year later Henry followed suit, and the two then entered architecture school at MIT (Massachusetts Institute of Technology) together, though the course here was markedly different from their hands-on training with Woodward. The brothers must have found the required stylistic borrowing from the past somewhat uncongenial. After two years, they duly obtained the certificate needed to enable them to enter professional apprenticeships. Each enrolled with a distinguished Boston office: Henry with Shepley, Rutan & Coolidge, a successor firm to Henry Hobson Richardson, and Charles with Winslow & Weatherall and later with H. Langford Warren who, at the age of 24, was working in Richardson's office.

The anticipated career on the East Coast did not, however, develop. In 1893, the brothers decided to visit their parents, who had moved to Pasadena. Reaching California after a stop-over in Chicago, where the Japanese pavilion at the World's Columbian Exposition had captured their imagination, they found a building boom just beginning. This, and the immediate opportunity to design a house for a butcher friend of their father's, persuaded the brothers to settle and set up practice in Pasadena. Over the next twenty years or so they designed some 180 buildings, 70 of which still exist today.

Although the Gamble House, Pasadena (1908), which has become a centre for Arts and Crafts studies on the West Coast, is now their best-known work, this large bungalow house was not the basis of Greene and Greene's fame and success in California. Rather, it was in their many smaller single and two-storey houses, where the brothers succeeded in imparting a charm, a dignity, a quality to even the most modest, that they devised a working vocabulary that could be emulated and refined in commission after commission. This vocabulary comprised the use of garden courts, overhanging eaves, shingle siding –

The Kinney Kendall Building, Pasadena, California, 1896, from the *Pasadena Illustrated Souvenir Book*, 1903. Distinguished by the attention given to maximising natural light into the interior of the building and by the simplification of textural elements into a concentrated spandrel and cornice which strengthened the horizontality of the clean design, the Kinney Kendall Building, designed in the second year of the Greenes' youthful practice, represents one of the few commercial structures that the firm chose to design. Its strong, clean lines introduced into Pasadena's booming building era a dramatic departure from the historicism of its earlier buildings.

James A. Culbertson House, Pasadena, California, 1906. Following the rejection of historicism demanded by earlier clients and the embrace by the Greenes of simple geometrical forms, the Culbertson House represents a major turning point in the Greenes' personal architectural style while also reflecting the influence of Charles Greene's wedding trip to England the previous year.

above all, the expression of structure as sculpture, in which the coming together of two constructional elements creates a third condition, as in the work of Mackintosh, where the resultant form is something other than the mere sum of its constituent parts. The working out of this expressed vocabulary can be seen in the designs which the Greene brothers evolved, particularly over the two decades from the start of their Pasadena practice until World War I.

The first years were spent jettisoning the remnants of East Coast eclecticism, exploring the indigenous architecture of the California missions, and gradually returning to the direct disciplines of their earlier manual sensitivity training. Two years into their joint practice came the Kinny Kendall Building, Pasadena (1896), in which the use of bands of windows, the clever introduction of light into the heart of the plan and a generally horizontal feel in the

Central courtyard, Arturo
Bandini House, Pasadena,
California, 1903. Throughout
their career, Charles and Henry
Greene each referred back to the
Bandini courtyard plan as having
freed them from traditional plan
constraints and opened the doors
to their rambling, casual plan
forms, embracing the ouside
spaces as, in fact, rooms defined
with different materials. Arturo
Bandini, son of an early
California family, had come to
the brothers specifically
requesting a simple wooden
board and bat construction based
upon the hacienda courtyard
plans of his ancestors.

Van Rossem-Neill House,
Pasadena, California, 1903/1906.
Originally constructed with
clapboard sidings, the house was
considerably updated to the
Greenes' rapidly maturing
personal architectural
vocabulary, which is clearly
expressed here in the new entry
porch roof structure, projecting
timber construction, driveway
pergola and massive terrace walls
of clinker brick and granite
boulders.

disposition of the masses, gave hints of what was to come. In the Swan House,
Pasadena (1895), built for their first really affluent client, Greene and Greene's
bold design wholly rejected their patron's first desire for a pastiche of the day.
By 1900, they had cast off all the popular historicising styles. California, it
seemed, provided the environment for exploring the new; its architecture was,
according to Charles Greene writing in 1905, 'a cross between a California
mission and a Mississippi steamboat with a bit of everything in between.'
Bernard Maybeck and Irving John Gill thought differently, but they too, like
Greene and Greene, had their unique interpretations.

Following a honeymoon to England and Italy in 1901, Charles Greene produced a somewhat English Tudor design for the Culbertson House (1906),

their first truly Arts and Crafts work. The house was filled with the furniture of Gustav Stickley, from whom the Greenes were to draw that delight in pegs and dowels so characteristic of their constructional detailing. A house for Don Arturo Bandini (1903) in simple redwood boarding featured another aspect typical of Greene and Greene planning – the central courtyard with its 'embrace of outdoor space', a planning device of far-reaching influence. The Tichenor House (1904) provided an opportunity to explore the possiblities inherent in oriental forms and to continue the translation of functional forms into decorative elements.

Now began the accelerated development of the Greene and Greene formal vocabulary supported by the most loving and meticulous employment of materials – leaded glass, iridescent Tiffany glass, oak, ash, Honduras mahogany. The brothers remained in total command – never the slaves of system, they expressed their structure clearly but could bend or extend it at will, but only at *their* will. (As late as 1928, Henry was writing long letters to his client forbidding him from moving a partition even one inch without the express authority of his architect.)

This maturing Arts and Crafts idiom – unique, adaptable, but rigorously pursued – brought the brothers clients who wanted the Greenes' progressive but disciplined free style. One such was Theodore Thomas Irwin, whose 1905 house has recently been restored with the help of 150 contemporary sepia photographs taken as a record by Irwin. Other examples of these ultimate bungalows include the Freeman Ford House, with its intimate central court set back from the street behind a grove of orange trees, and the Robert Blacker House, the largest wooden Greene and Greene house, based on a U-shaped plan by Pasadena architect Myron Hunt, but executed by the brothers, whose reputation for earthquake-resistant structures had won them the commission.

Opposite page. Top: Duncan/Irwin House, Pasadena, California, 1900/1906. Originally designed by the Greenes in 1900 for Katherine M. Duncan as a modest, one-storey, residence developed around a small atrium. In 1906, the Greenes were commissioned by Theodore M. Irwin to add a complete second floor and to update the building to expressed timber design ideas that they were rapidly developing.

Opposite page. Bottom left: living room wall lighting fixture, Adelaide Tichenor House, Long Beach, California, 1904. Predated only by leaded lanterns for the Jennie Reeve House six months earlier, this second design by Greene and Greene for leaded stained glass interior lighting demonstrates the speed in refinement of their designs between 1903 and 1904. In form, the lines exhibit the grace of later work and principles which continued throughout their careers. The medallion form in the front panel, so familiar in many later Greene and Greene compositions, is the first use of that form by the Greenes and was derived from the Japanese tsuba or sword guard, inspired by Charles Greene's collection of antique tsubas.

Bottom right: upright desk for Adelaide Tichenor House, Long Beach, California, 1904. No other design so clearly depicts the transition in the Greenes' furniture from the linear influences of Gustav Stickley to the nuances of the Greenes' mature personal creations as the ash secretary desk for the Tichenor House. The soft, undulating curve and sculptured forms of the side panels, the 'lift' utilised in the drawer handles and door detail, and the use of express joinery and expressed pegs and screws as decorative elements were to become the primary identifiable characteristics of Greene and Greenes' mature furniture designs.

Right: Freeman A. Ford House, Pasadena, California, 1907. Ground floor plan. The central courtyard plan adopted in the Freeman Ford design is a refined statement of concepts derived from early California Spanish hacienda structures that first appeared in the Greenes' design for the Arturo Bandini House of 1903.

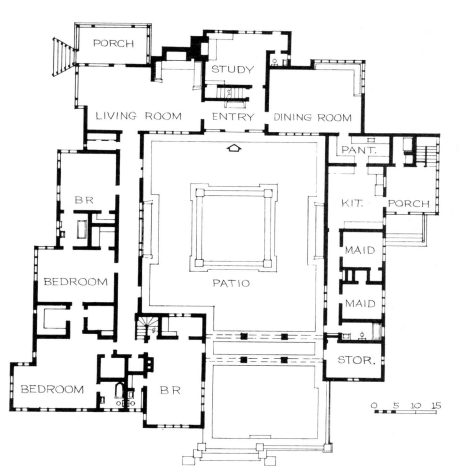

Central Courtyard, Freeman A.
Ford House, Pasadena,
California, 1907. Clearly related
to the Greenes' articulated,
timber-structured ultimate
bungalows, the Freeman Ford
House is representative of the
Greenes' most sophisticated and
genteel development of open and
free-plan forms which they felt
strongly were most appropriate
to the Southern California
landscape.

Below: outward view of the *porte-
cochère* of Robert R. Blacker
House, Pasadena, California,
1907. The Greenes' respect for the
structural detail of the Japanese
temple is seen in the construction
of the massive entry *porte-
cochère* of the Blacker House.
Clearly demonstrated is their
quest for the inter-relationship of
all parts of their designs: joinery,
lighting, structure, terrace,
gardens, seating, etc. No minor
detail was left to the discretion of
any craftsman. Every aspect of
design throughout their carers
was carefully conceived, and
each element looked upon as
though a part of a total painting.

In Charles Greene's own house, five different extensions give a concentrated
view of the brothers' design evolution. And, of course, there is the Gamble
House, with its beautifully preserved interiors fit to rival Mackintosh's library
at the Glasgow School of Art.

The partnership of Charles and Henry Greene was the perfect Arts and Crafts
collaboration. While both had had the same manual training and shared the
same hands-on philosophy, their separate talents and temperaments were precisely complementary. Charles, perhaps more imaginative, produced the
freer, more sinuous, naturalistic, almost Art Nouveau forms; Henry, more
linear or rectilinear in approach, brought discipline and order to their mutual
creation of a genuinely American Arts and Crafts architecture.

Above and below: Robert R. Blacker House, Pasadena, California, 1907. Front and rear views. The largest of the Greenes' fully mature, timber-structured residences, the Blacker House once exhibited the full spectrum of their talents. Careful attention was given to the design of every aspect of the interiors, furniture and furnishings as well as to the fully developed 5½ acres of gardens, including pergolas, koi pond, and garden pottery.

Through careful and creative shaping of the gardens and grounds, the Greenes made possible direct access from the main floor entry hall to the intimate rear terrace level and, at the same time, direct access to the garden and lawn area from the basement billiard room. The open and closed decks and sleeping porches of the two rear wings were positioned to have a panoramic view over the pond and the garden.

OLBRICH AND MACKINTOSH

Robert Judson Clark

★Letter, Olbrich to Claire Morawe, 1st November 1902 (private collection). Frau Morawe was recently divorced, and there was some question about where these official, but private vows should be exchanged.

★*See* Eduard F. Sekler, 'Mackintosh and Vienna' in *Architectural Review*, CXLIV, December 1968, pp.455-456; Roger Billcliffe and Peter Vergo, 'Charles Rennie Mackintosh and the Austrian Art Revival' in *Burlington Magazine*, CXIX, November 1977, pp.739-744.

Anticipating their forthcoming marriage, Joseph Maria Olbrich wrote in November 1902 from Darmstadt to his bride-to-be, Claire Morawe, in Dresden. 'It would be best if we were married in Glasgow,' he suggested. 'Thus, we could ask dear Mackintosh to listen attentively as we affirm our promise. He is the only one . . . who appears worthy to know first that we wish to follow together the law of nature in its enigmatic ways.'★

In fact, the couple merely travelled in April 1903 to the *Standesamt* in Wiesbaden. Nevertheless, these lines are a clue to something that goes beyond the immediate personal life of the 34-year-old architect from Vienna who was now practising in Darmstadt. Like many designers of his time, Olbrich was an admirer of Charles Rennie Mackintosh. Although Olbrich had left Vienna before the Mackintosh craze had begun there,★ he had been a judge in the 1901 *Haus eines Kunstfreundes* competition, which had helped to popularise Scottish Modernism on the Continent. If they had not done so before, Olbrich and Mackintosh met at the Turin exhibition of 1902. Their friendship was brief, but significant.

Olbrich and Mackintosh were contemporaries, the former born in December 1867 and the latter in June 1868. They were of the generation of architects who matured in the late 1890s and produced their best work in the first decade of the twentieth century, when they were affected, at least in part, by the tenets of the international Arts and Crafts movement. Both came from cities that were perceived by their young avant-garde as 'outposts' of European culture. Both had tragically short careers: Olbrich died suddenly of leukaemia in 1908, while Mackintosh lived another twenty years in relative inactivity.

Olbrich was trained in Vienna in the classical, academic tradition, while Mackintosh came out of the more northern, medieval heritage of Glasgow. Mackintosh soon emerged as an important figure in the 'free phase' of the late Gothic Revival. Olbrich, on the other hand, was ultimately true to the Classical ideals of his teachers, althogh he made important forays with work inspired by

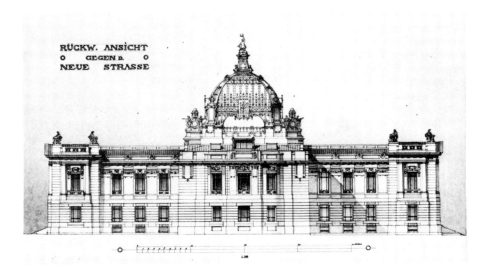

Project for Museum of Applied Arts, by Joseph M. Olbrich, Reichenberg, 1895. Rear elevation.

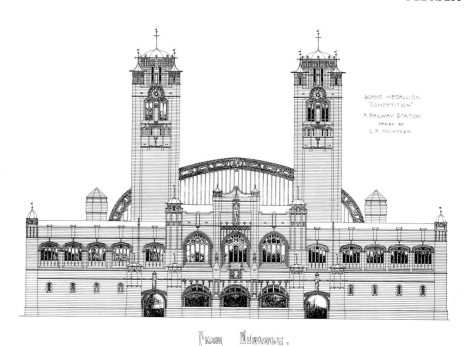

Project for Railway Terminal, by Charles Rennie Mackintosh, 1893.

*For further information on Olbrich's early career, *see* Robert Judson Clark, 'Olbrich and Vienna' in *Kunst in Hessen und am Mittelrhein*, VII, 1967, pp.27-51; R.J. Clark, 'Joseph Maria Olbrich and Vienna', unpublished Ph.D. dissertation, Princeton University, 1973.

the medieval vernacular. An example by each will suffice to underscore their early differences. As his Soane Medallion competition project of 1893 for a railway terminal, Mackintosh proffered a stylised neo-Gothic envelope out of which rises the profile of an arched train shed. In that same year, Olbrich entered the office of Otto Wagner, where he learned – and then helped to develop further – his master's vocabulary of a somewhat disjunctive Classicism and an enthusiasm for finely wrought flourishes of metal and glass. This modernised and decorative classical mode can be seen in Olbrich's own competition design of 1895 for the North Bohemian Museum of Applied Arts in Reichenberg, for which he received one of the two first prizes.*

The two young architects were very self-conscious in their development of a highly personal style of design and of graphic presentation. Mackintosh, however, early revealed a greater sense of abstraction. This can be seen in his

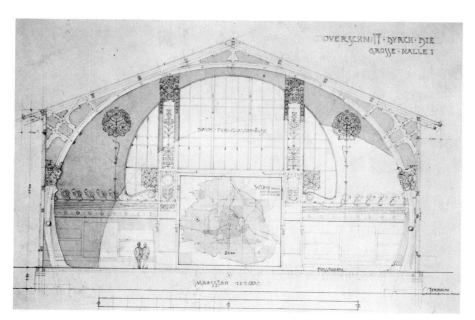

Project for Vienna Pavilion, 1897, for 1898 Jubilee Exhibition. Section.

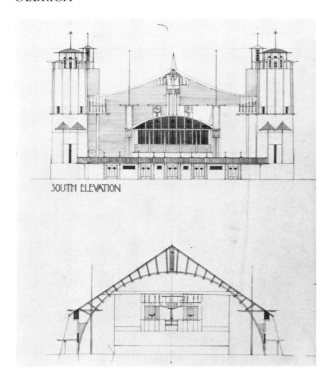

SOUTH ELEVATION

Above: project for Concert Hall by Mackintosh for 1901 International Exposition, Glasgow, 1898. Elevation and section. *Right:* project for Vienna Pavilion by Olbrich.

unexecuted scheme of 1898 for a concert hall, in which the novel architecture and the taut, spare delineations are of a consistent tenor. By contrast, Olbrich's façade and interior of 1897 for the Vienna Pavilion are complicated by painterly washes, bracketry, and visual puns. The total effect falters in its inadequate synthesis of convention and invention.

The joviality that radiates from Olbrich's drawings reflects his buoyant and energetic persona. He was a very social creature and quite naturally became one of the leaders of the Vienna Secession (founded in 1897) and the designer of its building, which was completed the following year. The simplified classicism of this structure, which was intended to last only ten years, was complicated by a plethora of 'modern' details, many of them inspired by English Arts and Crafts motifs as they were perceived by the anglophile avant-garde of Vienna. It was in this building that Mackintosh and his wife, Margaret Macdonald, were triumphantly received in 1900. The work they displayed here helped

Secession Building, Vienna, by Olbrich, 1897-98.

*Among recent publications that deal with Austrian turn-of-the-century modernism are Jane Kallier, *Viennese Design and the Wiener Werkstätte*, George Braziller, New York, 1986; Kirk Varnedoe, *Vienna 1900: Art, Architecture and Design*, Museum of Modern Art, New York, 1986.

Ernst-Ludwig-Haus, by Olbrich, Darmstadt, 1899-1900. Plan and photograph of front.

clarify the intentions of the Secessionists to create a modern decorative style in all the arts.★

But Olbrich missed these events of 1900 and experienced their aftermath only from afar. In September 1899, he had left Vienna and settled in Darmstadt, where he had been invited to join the Artists' Colony founded by the Grand Duke of Hesse, Ernst Ludwig. On the Mathildenhöhe, Olbrich revealed a new directness of conception in the Ernst-Ludwig-Haus studio building, which was designed and built in 1899-1900. This 'temple of work', with an entrance portal framed by a pair of gigantic figures symbolic of genesis, was Olbrich's first real masterpiece. Its plan was clearly revealed in its elevations. The long row of muntined windows lit the hallway that gave access to eight studios whose northern skylights were canted behind the brow of the façade.

Eight villas for artists and supportive friends of the Grand Duke were built on surrounding plots of the Mathildenhöhe. Seven of these were by Olbrich, whose style now ranged from an abstracted Mediterranean vernacular for the sculptor Ludwig Habich, to the decorative version of a Germanic farmhouse that Olbrich designed for himself. The experience of Darmstadt made an architect out of another of the colony's members, the painter and graphic designer Peter

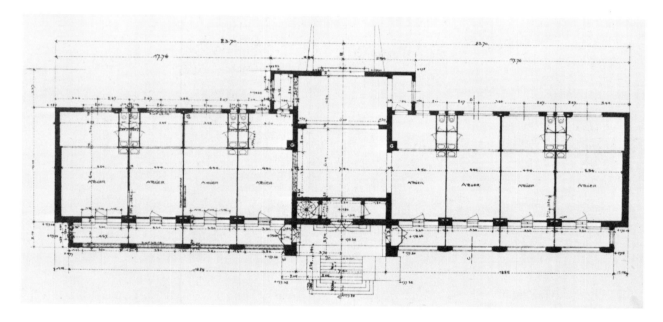

Behrens, whose more sombre house was preferred by many visitors to the 'Document of German Art', the exhibition that the colony held in 1901. One critic wrote: 'In the Behrens [music] room belongs the violin concerto of Beethoven with its stateliness; in Olbrich's rooms the rapturous music of, perhaps, Goldmark's *Queen of Sheba*.'★ The message was that on the Rhine seriousness and substance were more appropriate than colourful effects.

It was in this setting of artistic expectation and controversy that the forms of the mature Mackintosh house made their startling appearance, albeit on paper, in response to the 1901 international competition for a *Haus eines Kunstfreundes* – House of a Patron of the Arts, sponsored by Alexander Koch. Koch, who was born in Cologne and raised in Stuttgart, had married into the wallpaper manufacturing business. Settling in Darmstadt, he also became a publisher,

★Willy Seibert in the *Rheinische Musikzeitung*, XI, 21st June 1901, p.248, quoted in Fritz Hoeber, *Peter Behrens*, Munich, 1913, p.232.

Ludwig Habich house, by Olbrich, Darmstadt, 1900–01.

Below: house by Olbrich for himself, Darmstadt, 1900–01.
Below right: house by Peter Behrens for himself, Darmstadt, 1900–01.

Project by Mackintosh for a *Haus eines Kunstfreundes*, 1901.

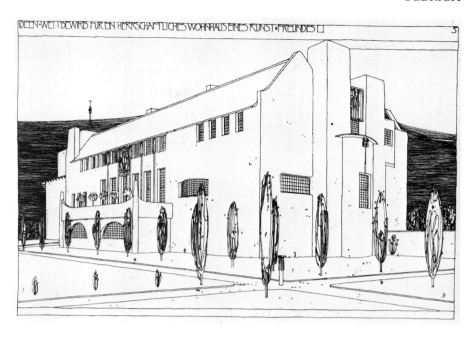

★The latter magazine was founded with the expressed intention of providing a German counterpart to *The Studio. See* Alexander Koch, 'An die deutsche Künstler und Kunstfreunde!' in *Deutsche Kunst und Dekoration*, I, October 1897, pp.i–ii.

★'Ideen-Wettbewerb', *Zeitschrift für Innen-Dekoration*, XI, December 1900, p.91a.

★Letter, Olbrich to Otto Wagner, 3rd November 1900 (private collection). Dülfer was never officially included.
★James D. Kornwolf, *M.H. Baillie Scott and the Arts and Crafts Movement*, Johns Hopkins Press, Baltimore, 1972, pp.216–238 (section based largely on information supplied by Clark, *see* p.234, no. 86).

★'Entscheidung des Wettbewerbes zur Erlangung von Entwürfen für ein herrschaftliches Wohnhaus eines Kunst-Freundes' in *Zeitschrift für Innen-Dekoration*, XII, July 1901, pp.111–113.

and founded, among other magazines, the *Zeitschrift für Innen-Dekoration* in 1890 and the more influential and broadly focused *Deutsche Kunst und Dekoration* in 1897.★

The *Haus eines Kunstfreundes* competition was announced by Koch in the December 1900 issue of *Innen-Dekoration*. Designs were to be for a grand country house of many rooms, with space for musical performances. Submitted drawings were to include three perspective sketches of interiors, for Koch, it must be remembered, was principally interested in wallpapers and furnishings. All was to be in 'a thoroughly modern style'. The instructions encouraged architects to co-operate with 'decorative artists of modern tendencies' in preparing their designs. Twelve judges were announced. Although Olbrich and Koch already harboured a mutual antipathy, the former was asked to join the panel. Eleven other judges were announced including Hans Christiansen (a painter and member of the colony), Henry Van de Velde, Otto Wagner and Koch.★

Olbrich wrote to Wagner in November 1906: 'I just want to tell you that I shall agree to assume the office of a juror in the competition sponsored here by A. Koch *only with the understanding* that all of the judges on the list . . . be deleted except for [you] and Martin Dülfer. Therefore, the jury would be: Otto Wagner, Vienna; Martin Dülfer, Munich; J.M. Olbrich, Darmstadt . . . Of the whole group, only we three can intercede for the new art.'★ But Olbrich did not have his way.

The outcome of the competition has been clarified somewhat in recent years.★ Thirty-six entries that had been received by the deadline of 25th March 1901 were considered worthy of judgement. It is clear that the judges were disappointed by the results. They reported that 'without the participation of foreigners, the results of the competition would have been very questionable indeed.' The nature of the programme for a single-family house had evoked the best responses from Anglo-Saxon entrants. Surely the unawarded first prize would have gone to Mackintosh and his collaborator, his wife, Margaret Macdonald, had they not failed to include the all-important interior perspectives. Instead, a special purchase prize was allotted them, with the following comment: 'Among several works that could not be considered with the finalists owing to violations of the rules of the programme, the design with the motto *Der Vogel* . . . especially stands out because of its pronounced personal quality, its novel and austere form, and the unified configurations of interior and exterior.'★

The second (and highest) prize went to M.H. Baillie Scott, whose plan and interiors were considered outstanding, although the exterior was 'not modern

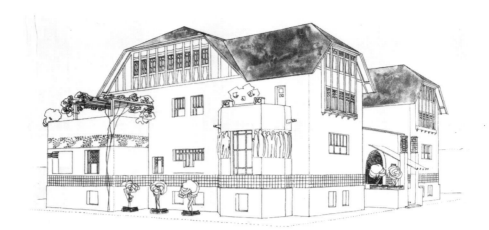

Project by Leopold Bauer for a
Haus eines Kunstfreundes, 1901.

Project by Paul Zeroch for a
Haus eines Kunstfreundes, 1901.

Project by Zeroch for a *Haus
eines Kunstfreundes*. A music
room.

Project by F.W. Jochem and
V.C. Mink for a *Haus eines
Kunstfreundes*, 1901. Hall.

enough.' Three third prizes were awarded: to Leopold Bauer of Vienna, whose
design reflected the work of Josef Hoffmann and of Olbrich, to Oskar Mar-
morek, also of Vienna, and to Paul Zeroch of Koblenz, who had drawn a Germanic country villa with details in Jugendstil. Zeroch's perspective of the
music room typifies the popularisation in Germany of the forms of Van de
Velde – in contrast to the so-called 'Darmstadt style' of Olbrich, which appeared
in the entry by two of his studio assistants, F.W. Jochem and V.C. Mink.

Living room, by Olbrich,
International Exhibition of
Modern Decorative Art, Turin,
1902.

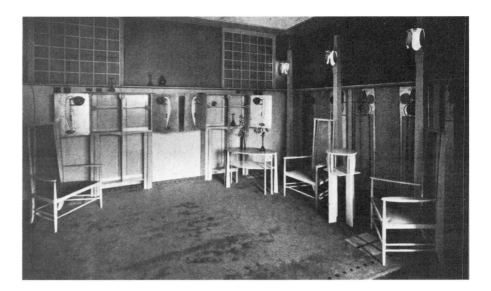

Room by Mackintosh,
Architectural Exhibition,
Moscow, 1902–03.

Dining room by Olbrich,
Architectural Exhibition,
Moscow, 1902–03.

★M.H. Baillie Scott, *Meister der Innen-Kunst, I: Baillie Scott, London: Haus eines Kunst-Freundes*, introduction by Hermann Muthesius; Charles Rennie Mackintosh, *Meister der Innen-Kunst, II: Charles Rennie Mackintosh, Glasgow: Haus eines Kunstfreundes*, introduction by Muthesius; Leopold Bauer, *Das Haus eines Kunst-Freundes: ein Entwurf in zwölf Tafeln von Leopold Bauer, Wien*, introduction by Felix Commichau (all Verlag Alexander Koch, Darmstadt, 1902). The interior perspectives by Mackintosh were drawn later in 1901 for his folio, hence the signature and dates, which would have been inappropriate for the competition.

★Letters, Olbrich to Claire Morawe, 10th May 1902 and 11th May 1902 (private collection).

★Letter, Olbrich to Claire Morawe, 2nd May 1902 (private collection), as quoted in Joseph August Lux, *Joseph M. Olbrich: eine Monographie*, Berlin, 1919, p.91.

Handsome portfolios of the *Haus eines Kunstfreundes* designs by Baillie Scott, Mackintosh and Bauer were published in 1902★ and were displayed in Koch's booth at the International Exposition of Modern Decorative Art in Turin that year. Elsewhere at the fair, one could see the latest interiors by Olbrich, which contrasted somewhat with his earlier work because of a new restraint in pattern and colour. Mackintosh was represented in Turin by a group of furniture arranged in a passageway. Olbrich reported to his fiancée: 'My three rooms are probably the best in the exhibition. . . . Mackintosh has also exhibited very well – but, alas, not really an interior.'★

As already mentioned, it is not known exactly when Olbrich and Mackintosh first met. But they socialised, together with other artist-friends, in Turin. Olbrich reported on 1st May 1902: 'In the evening I got together the Misters Berlepsch, Walter Crane, Mackintosh, etc., for a fine meal at the Restaurant Cambio. Afterwards, we were joined at our table by the Grand Duke [Ernst Ludwig], and we chatted until a quarter to eleven.'★

Works by Olbrich, Mackintosh and others could be compared several months later when the Grand Duchess Elizabeth, sister of Olbrich's royal patron, sponsored an exhibition of design in Moscow. Mackintosh's room was another arrangement of mostly pre-existing furniture, while Olbrich's dining room was an especially designed ensemble (with some silver objects added from his own house.) Joseph wrote to Claire about his confrontation with a Russian newspaperman; it revealed his continued respect for his Scottish colleague. 'Today a journalist came to [interview] me, but the fellow was so stupid that I simply could do nothing other than send him home like a donkey. Oh, this foolish critic – this dumb lamb allowed himself, in my presence, to make fun of Mackintosh's work.'★

The Darmstadt architect was invited to visit the Moscow School of Applied Arts. He was celebrated there in a manner somewhat like that which the Mackintoshes had experienced in Vienna a few years before. But Olbrich found it less than pleasant. 'The director and the faculty received me in the vestibule. It was too solemn to be able to laugh . . . Here, I am so highly regarded because of my work – more than a Persian shah by the Parisian demimonde. . . . The students were all standing around me in the corridor, to see the monster. The German students . . . had the nerve to give me a German ovation. That's when I wanted to walk away.'★

★Letter, Olbrich to Claire Morawe, 26th December 1902 (private collection).

★Letter, Olbrich to Claire Morawe, 29th December 1902 (private collction).

Dining room, by Olbrich, exhibition of the A.S. Ball furniture factory, Berlin, 1905.

Vestibule, by Alfred Grenander,
exhibition of the A.S. Ball
furniture factory, Berlin, 1905.

Below: Fountain Court by
Olbrich for the 1904 Louisiana
Purchase International
Exposition, Saint Louis, 1903–
04.

Project by Olbrich for railway station, Basel, 1903.

GROSSER GIEBEL DER HAVPTFASSADE FVR DEN NEVEN BAHNHOF IN BASE

Project by Mackintosh for Anglican Cathedral, Liverpool, 1903.

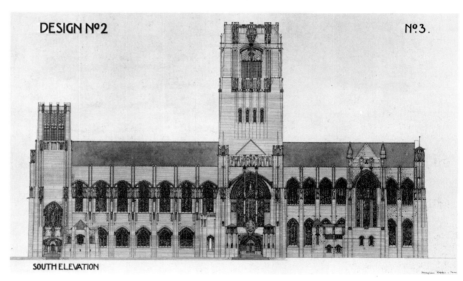

DESIGN N°2   N°3.

SOUTH ELEVATION

*Erich Haenel, 'Ausstellung der Dresdener Werkstätten für Handwerkskunst' in *Dekorative Kunst*, VII, January 1904, pp.146-167; Hans W. Singer, 'Arts and Crafts at Dresden,' in *The Studio*, XXXI, February 1904, pp.55-58.

*Max Creutz, 'Die Ausstellung von modernen Zimmer-Einrichtungen der Firma A.S. Ball' in *Berliner Architekturwelt*, VIII, April 1905, pp.25-28; Felix Poppenberg, 'Möbelausstellung' in *Kunst und Künstler*, III, April 1905, p.306.

*Letter, Olbrich to Claire Morawe, undated (private collection).

Later in 1903, works by Olbrich and Mackintosh were included in an exhibition at Dresden.* During 1903-05, the enthusiasm for Mackintosh's art continued to burgeon in Germany. This could be seen especially clearly in the pages of the *Berliner Architekturwelt*. In 1905, for example, there was an exhibition held in the Berlin showrooms of the A.S. Ball furniture factory. Most of the interiors revealed a startling debt to Mackintosh, including the dining room by Olbrich, and even more so the rooms by Alfred Grenander, the Swedish-born Berlin architect who had organised the event. Much less like Mackintosh's previous work was the room by Mackintosh himself, which was in dark tones, rather than white,* and very rectilinear.

By this time, it seems, there was no more direct contact between Olbrich and Mackintosh. The circumstances remain mysterious; an undated letter simply states, 'Today I also thanked Mackintosh without great feeling, but politely.'* Nevertheless, Olbrich's most important work of 1904, the Fountain Court at the Louisiana Purchase Exposition in Saint Louis, owed something to the stuccoed, white-washed exteriors and casement windows of Mackintosh. The quiet pools and tiled roofs injected a Mediterranean air. It was referred to as the court of a house of a patron of the arts, surely an indirect reference to Alexander Koch's competition of 1901.

The rest of Olbrich's *oeuvre* is characterised by a greater sense of monumentality and a renewed exploration of historical – mostly classical – forms. As

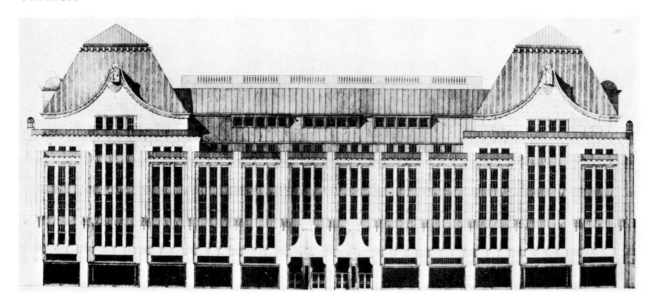

Leonhard Teitz Department
Store by Olbrich, Düsseldorf,
1906–09.

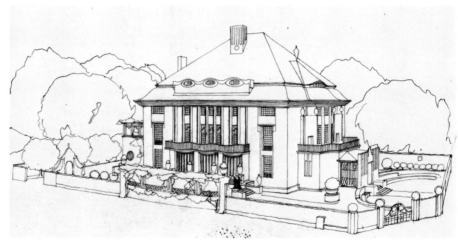

Project for Eduard
Schwarzmann house by Olbrich,
Strasbourg, 1905.

Joseph Feinhals house by
Olbrich, Cologne-Marienburg,
1908–09. Garden front.

*Especially the Basel station of 1906-13 by August Stürzenacker, and a project of 1905 by Rudolf Bitzan for that same competition.

*For example, the Karstadt department store on the Hermannplatz, Berlin, completed in 1929, by Philip Schaefer, who had worked in Olbrich's studio.

*Robert Judson Clark, 'The German Return to Classicism after Jugendstil' in *Journal of the Society of Architectural Historians*, XXIX, October 1970, p.273.

*Max Creutz, 'Das Haus Feinhals in Cöln-Marienburg' in *Dekorative Kunst*, XX, November 1911, p.69.

*On the covers of the 1960 and some subsequent paperback editions of Sir Nikolaus Pevsner's *Pioneers of Modern Design* are juxtaposed photographs of the Eiffel Tower, the Wedding Tower, the Library Wing of the Glasgow School of Art, and a detail of the Factory Administration Building, Cologne, by the ultimate hero of Pevsner's book, Walter Gropius.

early as 1903, his competition drawings for the railway station in Basel, for which he received the third prize, were enlivened by engaged columns, fluted piers, swags and figural sculpture. This would have been Olbrich's greatest building, had it been built. It was a most influential conception and inspired other German railway architecture for several years afterwards.* In the context of this paper, the Basel project should be compared with the exactly contemporaneous competition design by Mackintosh for the Anglican cathedral in Liverpool. In both, we see exquisite passages of inventive detail.

Olbrich, who was a lapsed Roman Catholic, never designed a church. But he referred to his largest constructed building the Leonhard Tietz Department Store in Düsseldorf, as 'his cathedral'. This structure was the result of a lengthy competition in 1906-07 and was completed in 1909, a year after the architect's death. It was a huge mercantile palace with vertically articulated bays and figured gables against a high mansard roof, all enclosing six floors and three light courts. This was very effective street architecture, as well as fine commercial space, and it became the model for many other designers who varied its themes for many years in the Rhineland and elsewhere – even in Berlin, where the work of Alfred Messel had originally inspired it.*

A series of houses that Olbrich designed between 1905 and 1908 shows a gradual, but decided, turn to a volumetric architecture that was classical in its repose and in many of its details. There is nothing like these buildings in the work of Mackintosh. The project for Eduard Schwarzmann in Strasbourg, unfortunately, remained unbuilt. Its plan went far beyond anything that Olbrich had attempted before on a domestic scale. Its sequence of spaces was probably inspired by the Germanic adaptations of Anglo-Saxon houses that were then being done in and near Berlin by the ultimate German anglophile, Hermann Muthesius, who was the key to so much of the British-German artistic exchange in these years.

These last houses by Olbrich culminated in the villa for Joseph Feinhals in Cologne, which was designed in 1908 and completed posthumously the following year. Feinhals was a proud citizen of this Rhenish city, but, like Olbrich, he was also a devoted Italophile. Strains of Germanic Classicism and references to Mediterranean sources were melded in a telling *tour-de-force*. The house was brought to completion by Bruno Paul, who, like his and Olbrich's contemporary, Peter Behrens, was a leader in the German return to Classical forms around 1905-10.* This change represented not only a search for more architectonic values, but also a rejection of what was seen as an inappropriate dependence on British and Franco-Belgian ideas of domesticity and the practical arts. According to an inscription intended for the main fireplace, the Feinhals house was to be a 'gesture toward the future . . . a testament of artistic longing amid years guided by a different persuasion.'*

The most famous of Olbrich's late works, but by no means his last, was the Wedding Tower of 1905-08 and its accompanying municipal Exhibition Building on the Mathildenhöhe. The series of exhibition spaces was in a simple classical style with German mansard roofs. The tower, which was commissioned by the citizens of Darmstadt to celebrate the second marriage of the Grand Duke in 1905, was constructed of clinker bricks in a slab form that recalled the towers of late medieval Germany. The rounded gables were a reference to the Germanic, shaped gables that in turn echoed those of north Italian Renaissance architecture. The whole complex is therefore a spirited blend of the medieval and Classical, of north and south.

It is appropriate that this remarkable composition in Darmstadt be compared with the library wing of Mackintosh's Glasgow School of Art, which was completed at about the same time.* While Olbrich's tower and galleries were commissioned separately, they were built in one campaign. Yet they retained a sense of being additive, a somewhat haphazard union. By contrast, Mackintosh's building, conceived as a whole but built in two stages over ten years, became, even with its intervening changes, an audacious whole. One might venture here to adapt and paraphrase Olbrich's remarkable letter of November 1902: Mackintosh is the worthy one.

Wedding Tower and Exhibition
Building by Olbrich, Darmstadt,
1905-08.

Library Wing, by Mackintosh,
Glasgow School of Art, 1907-09.

ILLUSION AND REALITY: FORM AND FUNCTION IN MODERN FURNITURE, c.1900
Christian Witt-Dörring

*J.A. Lux, *Die moderne Wohnung und ihre Austattung*, Vienna-Leipzig, 1905, p.18.

In 1905, Josef August Lux described the appearance of the majority of contemporary Viennese middle-class apartments as follows: 'Most still strive for the falsity of a counterfeit luxury, putting illusion above reality.'*

The situation is no different today: the less well-off continue to want to emulate the rich; their surroundings are designed to show off a superior social status, even where this is non-existent. The home exhibits features belonging to a more opulent lifestyle that are meant to give an illusion of elegance and grandeur. But where the means are lacking, one finds only reflections, suitably reduced in size, and cheap *ersatz* materials to conjure up an atmosphere of otherwise unattainable luxury.

The formal repertory of nineteenth-century historicising styles made it possible to accomplish such illusions by providing the means of furnishing in a style reminiscent of those previously only accessible to the top stratum of society. The lavishness which had been essential, but which the middle classes could not afford, was superficially achieved at the expense of the materials used. Cheap imitations and machine-made ornament brought about a decline in taste.

*J. Folnesics, *Unser Verhältnis zum Biedermeierstil*, Vienna, 1903, p.3.

During the 1890s, Europe's younger generation of artists became aware of this and began to seek a new, contemporary style. Vienna was particularly influenced by William Morris's socio-political ideas that had spread from England, among them an equation of beauty with utility and the demand for simplicity and genuineness. Vienna now began to identify itself with the last period when objects created by man had expressed a wholly integrated stylistic taste,* and it sought to retrace its steps to a time when suitable formal solutions had been found to the demands for functional and useful objects that came from the pressures of daily life. Such an integration of object and purpose seemed to have been accomplished by the penultimate generation, that of the artists' grandparents, the period officially and retrospectively recognised by 1900, among other distinct styles, as 'Biedermeier'.* This was a time when objects

*Kunstgewerbeblatt NF, Leipzig, 1900, vol. XI, p.124.

of daily life in Austria were not yet factory-made; during the early part of the nineteenth-century, the properties of raw materials were respected, with design and craftsmanship in the same hands. It was not until industrial production made the division of labour the rule, and design became subordinate to the machine, that the craftsman turned into a mere machine hand. Objects in daily use lost all individuality and style, a loss which also began to be felt in other aspects of daily life. William Morris was one of the earliest thinkers to see this connection, which led him to seek a revitalisation of ancient guild structures under artistic leadership. Such ideas were equally influential in Vienna; they provided the stimulus towards a new, 'modern' crafts movement around 1900, which was to culminate in a lively creative dialogue between fine art and the applied arts. As Ludwig Hevesi commented as early as 1899 on the Winter Exhibition at the Österreichisches Museum für Kunst und Industrie:

'That several artists of note have again turned towards the applied arts is another welcome proof that at last the applied arts appear again to have a future.'*

*Kunst und Kunsthandwerk, Vienna, 1900, vol. III, p.3. 'We see the painter Jungo Charlemont take his first steps in furniture-making with his study furniture, varnished green and with polished iron mounts, for the Dornbach country house of Herr Philipp von Schöller.'

The decade before 1900 had led to a recognition in Vienna that a new spirit of the times demanded new forms, which had not only to be striking and imaginative, but also suitable for people's practical needs and such new technical achievements as the telephone, electric light and cooking by gas. But, at the same time, raw materials were to be respected in a return to older traditions of craftsmanship. Purely luxury goods, though, were to be ignored, for the emphasis was to be on educating the taste of the majority.

Otto Wagner was the first to promote this idea in Vienna, and, from 1894 onwards he taught it to his students at the Academy:

'Everything modern, created now, must be suitable for modern materials and the demands of contemporary life, if it is to be suitable for modern man; it must put our very own better, democratic, self-reliant and keenly aware philosophy into concrete form and show awareness of the colossal technical and scientific achievements as well as the pervasive practical nature of mankind – surely this goes without saying!'[1]

The furnishing of his own apartment in Vienna, at Köstlergasse 3, during 1898–99, gave him the opportunity to create modern furniture for the first time: simple, constructivist forms, which, given the textile furnishings of the rooms, still seemed grafted on to a luxurious nineteenth-century historicism. One great novelty, true to the motto 'Reality, not Illusion', was the importance given to the bathroom fittings and to the furnishing of the service rooms. The Telegraph Office, 1901–02, and the Post Office Savings Bank, 1904–06, were further consistent developments of this style. In both buildings, Wagner used pieces of factory-made bentwood furniture. Elegant proportions, the simplest geometrical ornamentation (wherever possible in accord with function), absolute mastery of raw materials, which were even used at times to differentiate between various functions – all this makes these two buildings prototypes of the functional office interior.

In 1897, Adolf Loos had returned from America and started a campaign against bad taste with a series of articles in the *Neue Freie Presse*. He was called a product of American culture by a contemporary writer, who described him as striving for 'appropriateness and simplicity which when combined with first-rate craftsmanship, result in a natural, technical elegance.'[2]

This 'natural' result is the secret of Loos's interior decoration. Without wishing to impose his own creative invention on an object, Loos, like Otto Wagner, tried to combine form, function and material by the simplest means. He vehemently criticised the endeavours of the crafts movement to create complete dwellings together with their furnishings in one go, thereby limiting the personal freedom of their owner.[3] Otto Wagner was the only artist to whom he allowed such liberty.[4]

The impression that America made on Loos cannot be overestimated. In America, functional solutions to interior decoration and furniture making, then unknown in Vienna, had already been found.[5] Loos's 1898 designs for the furnishings of the gentlemen's outfitters Goldman & Salatsch clearly show the influence of American 'craftsman furniture' such as that made by Gustav Stickley in New York. Equally important was his relationship to England, whose traditionally self-confident middle class had created its own lifestyle which aimed for comfort rather than show – a lifestyle even imitated by the aristocracy. Loos used not only English types of chair, which he saw as ideal for their purpose, but also the 'cosy corner' and chimney-corner seating and adapted the living-room hall with its integral staircase from the English country house to form part of Viennese interior decoration.

Loos was supported in this enthusiasm by the newly appointed director of the Österreichisches Museum für Kunst und Industrie. In the 1897 Winter Exhibition, Arthur von Skala showed a great many examples of English and American seating and other small furniture, modern but following older models, which were to cause a positive mania in Vienna for furnishing in the English style. The following year, he exhibited the latest work by students of English schools of art and design.

It was in his Museum Café, 1898–99, that Loos showed his so-called *Nutzkunst* – 'Art for Use' – for the first time. Here he achieved an atmosphere of sober elegance without going to any great expense. Electric lighting, then

[1] O. Wagner, *Die Baukunst unserer Zeit*, Vienna, 1914, p.39.

[2] *Kunst und Kunsthandwerk*, Vienna, 1899, vol. II, p.196.

[3] In his parable 'of a poor, rich man', Vienna, 26th April 1900, Loos attacks the 'total work of art' in interior decoration.

[4] A. Loos, *Sämtliche Schriften*, Vienna, 1962, vol. I, p.46f.: 'I am against the movement which thinks it particularly excellent that a building should have been designed by one architect down to the last coal shovel . . . This destroys all character and originality. But I must admit that I capitulate before the genius of Otto Wagner, for he has a talent I have hitherto only found in one or two English architects: he is capable of slipping out of his architect's skin and into that of some craftsman. Let him create a glass – he will think like a glass blower, a glass polisher . . .'

[5] Contemporary architectural journals were full of articles and descriptions of American country houses and their so-called 'patent furniture'.

Stool by Otto Wagner for the banking hall of the Austrian Post Office Savings Bank in Vienna, 1906. Beech, stained brown, aluminium fittings. Made by the Thonet brothers.

Cupboard by Sigmund Jaray from a suite of furniture for a married worker, 1899. Elm, with iron fittings.

Chair by Adolf Loos for the Museum Café in Vienna, 1899. Beech, stained red, cane seat. Made by J. & J. Kohn.

★*Kunst und Kunsthandwerk*, Vienna, 1898, vol. I, p.60.

quite new, was distributed throughout the space sensibly and simply by means of plain bulbs. The seating furniture, by Kohn, was made from bentwood and constructed by him personally so as to give the right weight distribution. The tables were from the Kohn factory catalogue, the billiard tables from the old-established Viennese firm of Seifert. The design was a mixture of purpose-built objects and existing ones, long proven in use – there was no question of a forced formal unity being imposed on this interior. We find the same characteristics in Loos's interior decoration for private houses.

Loos's creations formed a sharp contrast to the formal renaissance which was taking place all over Europe in reaction to nineteenth-century historicism. Masquerading as a second Renaissance, the new styles of plant ornamentation had been applied to traditional furniture types and had been put before the buying public as modern and functional furnishing. Vienna's first sight of such a 'modern, functional' interior, in which 'graceful and yet logical forms are adapted, as far as possible, to today's functionalism'★ had been at the Öster-reichisches Museum für Kunst und Industrie in 1897. The exhibit in question was a ladies' drawing room created by the architects Josef Urban and Franz Schönthaler Jr. in collaboration with the painter Heinrich Lefler and the sculptor Hans Rathausky. This was what Adolf Loos thought about it:

Ladies' Drawing Room by Josef Urban, Franz Schönthaler and Heinrich Lefler, in the Winter Exhibition at the Österreichisches Museum für Kunst und Industrie, Vienna, 1897.

★Loos, 1962, vol. I p.149.

★J. Folnesics, *Das moderne Wiener Kunstgewerbe* in *Deutsche Kunst und Dekoration*, Darmstadt, 1900, vol. VI, p.256.

★*Das Interieur*, Vienna, 1900, vol. I, p.17 ff, p.177 ff.

★*Der Architekt*, Vienna, 1897, p.13.

'It certainly looks modern. But have a closer look and you will see our dear old German Renaissance fancy-dress room with a modern top-dressing. Nothing is missing. The wood panelling complete with factory-applied wooden intarsia inlay, the medieval German decorative divan (may God rest its soul!) . . .'★.

In Vienna, the trend in the use of these modern forms was pursued by a number of young artists from the ranks of the Secession who were keen to follow the new demands for up-to-date functional forms created in materials appropriately used. Josef M. Olbrich's 1899 Spitzer Apartment showed a very personal style in interior decoration, reminiscent of contemporary painting in its colouring. His furniture types represent a 'modern baroque', as J. Folnesics acutely remarks.★ A preponderance of constructivist elements is intermingled with Secession-type decorative and structural elements. The bathroom of the Spitzer Apartment is a particularly striking example of this blend of styles. In the interiors of his Vila Bahr (1899-1900), the Secession elements are already dwindling in comparison with the constructivist ones.

Robert Örley expressed his views about functional furniture in two programmatic articles published in 1900★. In them he repeats the usual demands. What is interesting, though, is the way in which he put them into practice – for example, his extremely functional seating with woven straps is reminiscent of Richard Riemerschmid. What were particularly new were the cupboards and stools, which look as though they have been roughly nailed together from planks.

But the future development of the modern Viennese interior was due far more to Josef Hoffmann and Kolo Moser and their students in the College of Applied Art than to Josef M. Olbrich and Robert Orley. Josef Hoffmann's demand that interiors should be 'total works of art' (like Wagner's operas) was at the opposite pole to the ideas of Adolf Loos. As early as 1897, Hoffmann postulated 'that here, too, one day the hour will come when wallpaper and ceiling decoration, like furniture and everyday objects, will be ordered not from a shop, but from an artist.'★ Thus, he prepared the ground for a rethinking of the relationship of man with everyday objects. He stripped them of their

Stool by Josef Hoffmann from a suite of kitchen furniture for a shooting lodge, Bergerhöhe, 1899. Softwood, painted white. Maker unknown.

*L. Hevesi, 'Die Winterausstellung im Österreichischen Museum', in *Kunst und Kunsthandwerk*, Vienna, 1900, vol. III, p.11.

Part of a suite of bedroom furniture by Josef Hoffmann for Ernst Stöhr's studio house in St Johann am Wocheinersee, 1898. Softwood, stained green. Maker unknown.

anonymity by striving towards a close contact between the customer, the designer and the craftsman. In England, this kind of collaboration was already in existence. Fired by the ideas of Ruskin and Morris, C.R. Ashbee had founded the Guild of Handicraft. This was the instrument which had enabled him to create objects, perfect according to his views, in close contact with craftsmen and deeply conscious of the properties of the materials used. Not only was this craft community the model for the Wiener Werkstätte (founded in 1903), but the applied arts in Vienna were strongly influenced by the forms it created, particularly by the constructivist elements in Ashbee's furniture (which was also strongly reminiscent of medieval forms). The Wiener Werkstätte was equally strongly influenced by the social thinking that was deeply embedded in the English crafts movement; the craftsman was to become an integral force in the process of creation – his work was to give joy. It was a visible indication of this attitude that the various craftsmen were encouraged to punch or sign their work with their initials or names.

Hoffmann's earlier furniture, from before 1900, is characterised, like Örley's and Olbrich's, by floral decorative motifs and a sense of movement which, however, remains purely two-dimensional. This sense of movement is created through circles and segments cut out of boards, or through their shaping in such forms. The various elements are joined according to constructivist principles and have the characteristics of the so-called *Brettelstil* ('board style'),* leading to modern, functional furniture with a social purpose. Among these early works is the interior decoration of the House on the Bergerhöhe and the Secretary's Office at the Vienna Secession (1898-99). The furnishing of the painter Kurzweil's studio, shortly before 1900, was still part of Hoffmann's early work, but here the separate structural elements are already beginning to merge into a single whole. A dining-room interior shown at the Österreichisches Museum's Winter Exhibition in 1899 presents, as it were, a first step in this direction, although it still exhibits floral decorative elements.

It was Hoffmann's furniture show at the Eighth Exhibition of the Secession in 1900 which represented his unmistakable breakthrough towards a functional form, bare of ornamentation. It put into practice solutions that Adolf Loos had already pioneered. The usual view, that so-called 'functional forms' were first represented in Vienna by the objects from Scottish artists (Charles Rennie Mackintosh and Margaret Macdonald) shown at the Eighth Exhibition of the

★'Die VIII. Ausstellung der
Wiener 'Secession' in *Die
Kunst*, München, 1901, vol. IV,
p.176.

Secession, can now be seen to be false, in the light of earlier interiors created in
Vienna. It was rather a case of the typical Scottish line, already known in Vienna,
having influenced earlier Viennese furniture. ★ But it was true that the first
showing of the Scottish artists in Vienna led to more sensitive forms and proportions in Viennese furniture, as well as an awareness of new uses of colour in
interior decoration.

Kolo Moser showed the first pieces of furniture from his own designs at the
Secession in 1900. These included the famous dining-room sideboard with his
characteristic surface ornamentation ('The abundant draught of fishes'). His
contemporaries praised his work as the most successful. ★

Seat by Josef Hoffmann for the
hall of Dr Hans Salzer's flat in
Vienna, 1902. Beech and
softwood, painted white. Maker
unknown.

Desk by Kolo Moser for
Fritz Wärndorfer, 1903.
Makassar ebony veneer,
marquetry in Madagascan
ebony, box, mahogany, ivory
and tortoiseshell, brass fittings.
Made by Wiener Werkstätte.

★W. Fred, 'Die Wiener
Sezession: VIII. Austellung' in
*Kunstgewerbliche Zeitschrift für
Innendekoration*, February 1900,
p.32: 'The relations of the side
pieces to each other, of the
cupboard to the upper part, the
slight curve of the top – all these
are delicate details of
construction which, at the same
time as they make a piece of
furniture more functional, make
it appeal to our feelings . . .'

Tea table from furniture for the flat of Dr Hermann Wittgenstein, 1905. Oak with veneer, stained black, inlay of black marble with white vein. Made by Wiener Werkstätte.

Stool by Wilhelm Schmidt, 1901-02. Elm, brass screws, cane seat. Made by Prag-Rudniker.

*A. Loos, *Das Andere, Ein Blatt zur Einführung abendländischer Kultur in Österreich*, Vienna, 1903, 1-2, p.2.

True to the credo of the Modern Movement, which hoped to provide the middle classes, too, with daily objects 'as tasteful as they were functional', Kolo Moser and Josef Hoffmann and their students also provided designs for mass production (Prag-Rudniker Korbwaren, Kohn, etc.).

The interiors created by Hoffmann and Moser after the Secession exhibition show the influence of the Scottish artists, particularly in the use of white sharply contrasted with another colour. Harmoniously proportioned pieces of furniture, simply but clearly constructed, were made to match, with sparse geometric ornament or else the 'Scottish line'.

This can be seen in Hoffmann's villas on the Hohe Warte (Moser-Moll, 1900, Spitzer, 1901-02, Henneberg, 1901) and various apartment interiors (Dr Salzer, 1902, Biach, 1902). Through the collaboration of Hoffmann and Moser, the newly founded Wiener Werkstätte was instrumental in carrying through integrated projects including Sanatorium Purkersdorf (1904-5) and the Brussels Palais Stoclet (from 1905).

Towards 1910, though, the simple, clear form that had originally been advocated by Hoffmann began to recede and the influence of the Wiener Werkstätte led to a decorative style in a refined taste. The hopes of achieving a truly contemporary, functional artistic style before the turn of the century in Vienna had once again been set at naught by the motto, 'Decorate your home, but this time do it tastefully.' Only Adolf Loos had remained true to his principles in the timeless elegance of his creations. This circular development may be concluded with his words that were once more becoming relevant:

'. . . There was a time when there was no difference between English and Austrian furniture and the products of the carpenter's shop. That was the time of the Vienna Congress, a time almost one hundred years ago, when almost every force was at work to reduce us slowly, but surely, to the level of the inhabitants of some Balkan republic.'*

ÖDÖN LECHNER AND HIS FOLLOWERS: HUNGARIAN ARCHITECTURE, c.1900

János Szirmai

I regard it as an honour that Ödön Lechner should be ranked alongside Charles Rennie Mackintosh and his turn-of-the century contemporaries – an honour to the man himself and also to Hungarian architecture. On both counts, I believe it to be well merited: Lechner's work broke the historicising mould of the immediate past by seeking out and reviving national culture, and subsequently Hungarian architecture has, except for short periods, continued the search for a national building style and has treasured the memory of its great proponent.

In 1928, leading artists and critics, contemporaries and direct followers of Lechner, joined together to found the Ödön Lechner Society to preserve folk art and a spirit of genuine national endeavour. Much later, after the demise of the historicist architecture that had been created by dogmatism in the early 1950s, a Lechner monograph was among the first studies to fill the gap.

The first evaluation of the history of Hungarian attempts to create national forms was, however, published in 1929 to help raise funds for an Ödön Lechner statue. Its author, Béla Jánszky, belonged to an eminent group of adherents of the movement towards a national architecture which had unfolded in the wake of Lechner's activity. Lechner, indeed, was no isolated phenomenon like Antoni Gaudí. He was responsible for a breakthrough that allowed a fresh breeze to flow into the life of Hungarian society and culture. His work was taken up by an increasing number of followers, resulting in an internationally important development in architecture. Rather than dealing with Lechner alone, I should like to examine the main trend in which Lechner clearly had a decisive part. I shall not attempt to be comprehensive in dealing with his contemporaries or their buildings, but I shall try to demonstrate what was progressive in the traditions respected by the outstanding architects of the period and what was international in their national endeavours. To make myself clear, I first need to look briefly at Hungarian history.

After several centuries of migration starting in the Ural region, the Magyar people settled in the Carpathian basin in east-central Europe by the end of the ninth century. This area was already the meeting point of great powers and cultures. The western part was for a time the Roman province Pannonia, bounded by the Danube. The geopolitical situation of this territory governed the course of its history for many years. Even the Hungarian royal crown has two parts: one donated by the Pope, the other by the Emperor of Byzantium. This area was also where the Mongol invasion of the thirteenth century ended, for, over a long period, Hungary remained a bulwark of Christianity against Islamic expansion. In 1526, however, the Turks won a decisive victory at Mohacs, depriving the country of its independence and sovereignty for several hundred years, as a century and a half of Turkish rule was followed by the long era under the Hapsburgs, which lasted until the end of World War I.

Hapsburg oppression so affected the nation that members of all social classes took part in the struggle for independence which came to a head in 1848-49. Armed uprising was, however, accompanied by political struggle, and this so-called Reform period also saw a modern literary language beginning to develop, and a blossoming of literature and the arts. In architecture, this was the age of Classicism, imitating, of course, the architecture of the ancient democracies.

In the two dark decades following the repression of the War of Independence, the arts were considered essential to reinforce national consciousness, and scholarship was much engaged in investigations into the origins of the nation. These factors underlay both the first architectural experiment by Frigyes Feszl to create a national style and the work of Ferenc Liszt, the Hungarian composer and pioneer of modern music. Some surviving designs by Frigyes Feszl still bear the description 'Hungarian style'. His conscious endeavour was, however, opposed not only by political power but also by lesser artists: his style was stamped 'impure', and his work castigated as 'lacking a style'. In 1865, after the completion of the Municipal Concert Hall, Budapest, his most typical work, no major project was commissioned from him. The Concert Hall is symbolic in two ways: first, it is a liberal re-building of the previous Classical hall, which before its destruction by the Austrians in the War of Independence, had been one of the meeting places of nobles and citizens of Pest-Buda, who were partisans of independence; second, as a result of the scholarly researches of the time, its architecture has a strongly national character. By then, it was already known that the Magyar people originated from the east, but little more had been discovered. Feszl, applying Byzantine and Moorish motifs alongside Romanesque ones, was convinced that these oriental styles somehow represented the arts of his ancestors.

Two years later, in 1867, the *Ausgleich* with Austria came about – half-way independence, it was true, but nonetheless an important stage in the development of modern Hungary. The country battled to overcome its backwardness, striving to pattern itself after the advanced capitalist countries of Western Europe. In architecture, this was the age of historicism. National architecture appeared nowhere except at the Millennial Exhibition of 1896, where a retrospective collection of the history of Hungarian architecture was constructed.

Cultural policy, however, endorsed historicism as a national style demonstrating historical legal continuity and Hungarian leadership in a multinational country. By that time, however, the study of the popular arts had already produced important achievements, and the artist who became the standard-bearer in the fight for national character in the arts – Ödön Lechner – had appeared on the stage.

Rather than seeing Lechner as an isolated phenomenon it is instructive to regard him as representative of a widespread new European movement. His career began like that of his historicising contemporaries, his *oeuvre* being characterised by the search for a style – a Hungarian style. In this respect, he was, in fact, rather nearer to the academic mentality of which he was a convinced opponent than to turn-of-the-century trends. His chief merit was to have recognised the possibilities offered by new building materials and structures, and the necessity for an independent, national architecture. He strove to synthesise these two aspects, allowing his successors to adopt him as a model and progress further.

He studied in Budapest and in Berlin. In contrast to most of his Hungarian colleagues, he was primarily interested in new materials rather than in historical studies. In study tours abroad (mainly in France and in Great Britain), he was concerned to investigate whatever might be utilised in his architecture at home. For instance, in France, co-operating on the reconstruction of over thirty castles and palaces, he became aware of the stylistic adaptiveness of French Renaissance. This French influence is felt in his first works that point to a change: the Pension Office at the Hungarian State Railways building in Budapest (1883-84), with its coffee-house in the first two storeys, and the Thonet House, Budapest (1888-89). The Pension Office coffee-house chairs were ornamented with tulips, and the second storey ceiling painted in a mock-Hungarian manner. But, as he wrote in his *Sketch of an Autobiography*, published in 1911, 'I had to discover the impossibility of matching the primitive crudeness of Magyar folk art and sophisticated French culture . . .★

Lechner had rather a schematic knowledge of, and attitude to, Hungarian folk art. Rather than studying it himself, he turned to folk art studies published after Feszl's activity, especially Huszka's collection, which insisted on the continuity of Asian origins.

★Ödön Lechner, 'Önéletrajzi vázlat' (Sketch of an Autobiography) in *A Ház* (The House), 1911, pp.344-346.

On the other hand, he was well acquainted with building materials. while still a boy, he had helped in the work of his father's brick factory in the Kőbánya suburb of Pest, where he became familiar with ceramics, and he later delighted in the Asian collection of the museum in South Kensington during his second, longer study trip to England (1889). (By coincidence, the aged Feszl had also retired to Kőbánya, making contact between the two families a strong possibility.) In London, his views on the importance of building materials were matched by those on the significance of a distinctly national style. He observed, during his stay in Britain, that just as the great cultural nations were concerned with the historical and popular traditions of their colonial territories, 'all the more so are we Hungarians bound to study the art of our people and to fuse it with our general European culture.' Since the architecture of the Eastern peoples was 'raised to a certain monumentality,' this, Lechner argued, could help 'to translate popular elements into monumental architecture.'★

★Lechner, 1911.

The Thonet House had featured majolica and glazed tiles, and these became identifying features of his architecture after his second London journey. He travelled in the company of Vilmos Zsolnay, at that time head of the Zsolnay chinaware factory, a family business which had achieved world fame by the invention of eosin glaze. It was then that a creative collaboration was established between the two men, as a result of which the factory in Pécs supplied building ceramics not only to Lechner but to the growing number of adherents of an evolving national style. In fact, bricks and ceramics were traditional building materials in a country poor in stone, and so the struggle for a Hungarian style and the use of particular building materials became connected.

This process can be traced in the *oeuvre* of Lechner, in which the Town Hall, Kecskemet, completed in 1892, is the next building of note. A certain French character prevails, but only in part – the moulding of the mass has become more distinctive, and architectural ceramics applied on the roof and the cornices bear conventionalised, mainly oriental motifs.

If the first stage of Lechner's *oeuvre* comprises his early, historical buildings, it is in the second stage that the real foundations of a national style were laid. This second period ends with the Museum of Applied Arts, Budapest, built from 1893 to 1896. Giving up attempts to unite historical and national forms, Lechner now found building materials to fit a still more specifically Hungarian style (clinker, glazed tile, wrought iron), although, because of its new monumentality, this building, dubbed 'the palace of the Emperor of Gypsies', turned out perhaps a little too oriental in appearance.

Perhaps this is the building where Lechner was at his most style-bound. Exterior and interior have their own lives; inner functionality and environmental impact are greatly inferior to those of major European museums, including, ironically, the historicist Hungarian National Museum, built half a century earlier as a symbol of national independence. Now, however, Lechner became aware of the significance of the plan, and the relationship between function, structure and form. The exposed steel structure covering the central hall, after British models, introduced an architectural concept known elsewhere but new in the Hungarian context, though paradoxically it was meant to evoke ancestral tent interiors.

The Institute of Geology, Budapest, completed in 1899, points again to these changes in Lechner's architecture; the whole building emphasises questions of functionality rather than matters of symbolism or eastern origin – even ornaments now became increasingly functional.

His last great work, the Post Office Savings Bank, Budapest (1899-1901) 'unites the already modern with the Hungarian' – as one of his zealous critics put it in 1902.★ How did this undoubted qualitative change in Lechner's architecture come about? The narrowness of the plot inspired him to maximum land use, e.g. the central position of the counter hall in the courtyard. The narrow street required a new mass formation, while the need for inexpensive, fast construction and flexibility suggested the use of contemporary structures. From this starting point, he created a building that – like the work of Ludwig Mies van der Rohe – could be said to have 'skin and bones' architecture. In its

★Ödon Gerő, 'A Postatakarékpénztár Háza' (The House of the Post Office Savings Bank) in *Művészet* (Art), 1902, pp.41-55.

Post Office Savings Bank,
Budapest, by Ödön Lechner,
1899–1901.

plan and structure, it is the first representative of the pre-Modern Movement in Hungary, while its façade, decorated with symbolic and maturely conventionalised motifs, captures the essence of the Lechnerian style – called 'Lechnerism' by some. But just as the steel inside shines through the cover of the inner columns, the birth of a new architecture can also be felt behind the façade, the so-called 'Queen's kerchief'.

The interiors are mainly functional, particularly in rooms with no institutional purpose such as staircases and offices. Ornament designed by Lechner is restrained, a mere underlining to the spaces. The façades are original in themselves. Commonplace projections have been reduced to markings, not merely because of the narrow street but as a result of the general functional spirit of the building. Piers, especially at corners, are more structural – acting as tectonic, rather than stylistic symbols. Throughout the façade ornamentation, the principles of functionalism incipient in the Museum of Applied Arts have matured: ornamentation stresses the building's structure – openings, cornices, ridges, etc. Ribboned framing, typical of Lechner – in particular, on the crowning crenellations and ridges – is expressive of function. Yet the architect still had to ornament the roof with the symbol of the Post Office Savings Bank, a beehive, in yellow ceramic. Over the door is featured the famous bullhead motif, taken from the so-called 'Attila's Treasure', a sensational archaeological find of the time and seen as a symbol of the national past and the nation's right to sovereign statehood.

This work by Lechner brought him to the zenith of his career, a moment that could have marked a decisive point in Hungarian architecture. But it did not. In April 1902, the Minister of Public Education stated before Parliament: '. . . I dislike Art Nouveau, and, since often what is called Hungarian style is in fact Art Nouveau . . . I shall do my best to prevent it, I shall not equate it with the real Hungarian style . . .'* The minister certainly did not consider Lechner's

*Budapest Közlöny (Budapest Official Gazette), 18th April 1906, reprinted in Károly Lyka, 'Szecessziós stilus – Magyar stilus' ('Secessionist style – Hungarian style') in Művészet (Art) 1902, pp.164–180.

Post Office Savings Bank, Budapest, by Ödön Lechner, 1899-1901. Detail of crenel.

★Ödön Lechner, 'A magyar épitöstilusról' (About the Hungarian Architectural Style), delivered to the general assembly of the Szeged Dugonics Society, 1st June 1902, reprinted in Tibor Bakornyi-Mihály Kubinszky, *Ödön Lechner*, Corvina Press, Budapest, 1981, pp.181-183.

★B.F., 'A Szabadkai városháza' (The Szabadka Town Hall) in *Vállalkozók Lapja* (Contractors' Journal), 25th September 1912.

architecture 'real Hungarian style' and so, like Feszl, Lechner received no more major commissions. He had no opportunity to teach or to found a school. His concept of a master school based on practical work rather than on historical style studies, widely acclaimed and supported by his circle and followers, was ignored. The last decade of his life was spent in a struggle for the adoption of a Hungarian style and for the establishment of a master school. He was no revolutionary, but his campaign did result in some important papers and lectures.★ These again reflect the eclecticism of his artistic thinking: to achieve his goal, he adopted the highly charged nationalist ideas and phraseology of the formal politics of his time, so entering his name and his style in the service of the Magyar nationalist cause in the multinational Austria-Hungary. For instance, a paper on Szabadka Town Hall, built in Lechner's style in a territory of mixed nationalities, stated: 'Such a permanent building politically overrules quite a number of ministerial by-laws subject to temporal changes. Without any extraneous constraint, minorities will accept the Hungarian language in view of the superiority of Hungarian form and style . . . Several buildings of this kind are a better proof of the predominance of the Hungarian race than are Hungarian arms . . . This is the meeting place of citizens where they perform their civic duties. Seeing, feeling at any time that they are in a Hungarian building helps them to recognise and respect the force of Hungarian superiority!'★

However, Lechner did formulate the idea of a progressive Hungarian architecture, as is clear in his last paper, entitled 'Sketch of an Autobiography', written three years before his death: ' . . . a correct plan coping with living conditions and necessities, has now become of decisive importance, the starting point even.' Or: 'Everything that I have achieved up to now is by no means a fully accomplished work of art. On the contrary, all my works are experiments, their entirety is a stammer, a mere alphabet compared to the idiom in which a successor, an inspired artist, will create odes, hymns of fine art. But it will not take one man or two but even the co-operation of a generation. In effect, all I and my recent followers and friends have done is only the very beginning . . . But even if we could not do everything by ourselves, time will help us, the involuntary rule of development will work for us . . .'*

In 1911, the year of publication of this paper by Lechner, three buildings by Béla Lajta, landmarks in modern Hungarian architecture after the Post Office Savings Bank, were already being constructed. The process accomplished by these three buildings started partly with, and partly parallel to, the activity of Lechner. Its origins lie in ethnographic research and the wish to create a new Hungarian architecture, as well as in the other national architectural trends

Károly Kós: Project for a manor-house on a hillside, 1908.

126

underway around the turn of the century, in particular, in Britain and Finland. Lechner's followers were many. Those devoted principally to nationalist goals are joined by others interested solely in structure. Still others attempted to match 'Lechnerism' to European trends, especially Viennese Jugendstil. I must restrict myself here to the most creative promoters in this broad spectrum.

Patronage sprang from the radical bourgeoisie which had developed throughout nineteenth-century Europe, a class which already recognised contradictions in its social order, welcoming, but at the same time keeping in check any change because of its conflicting interests. The rise of this new stratum was strongly marked in Hungarian cultural life in the fifteen years between the turn of the century and the outbreak of World War I. Bourgeois and socialist ideas appeared simultaneously in literature, the fine arts, music and architecture, in parallel or interlaced.

The best known personalities of this historical and cultural period in Hungary are the folklorist-composers Béla Bartók and Zoltán Kodály, who performed the same task of collecting work in the field of folk music that had started earlier in the decorative arts and was paralleled in popular architecture. The slogan of Hungarian movements campaigning for an art of national character was taken from a Transylvanian ballad collected by Bartók and Kodály: 'Only from a pure source!'. While for Bartók this source was folk music irrespective of nation, his architect contemporaries considered it to lie in the origins of national architecture.

Ede Thoraczkai Wigand was the first to follow this path. Acquainted with popular architecture, he utilised its lessons not merely in the creative application of ornament, but, rather more significantly, in the restoration of a unity of form, structure and function. He was primarily an interior and industrial designer. Nevertheless, his environmental approach brought him in contact with architecture, and by the mid 1910s he had met up with the group known as 'The Young Ones'. Adopting a critical attitude to Lechnerian traditions, these architects and graduate students – Károly Kós, Béla Jánszky, Dezső Zrumeczky, Dénes Györgyi and others – addressed themselves both to popular architecture and to the influence of contemporary British movements. They did serious collecting work, above all in Transylvania, where folk art

Below: design by Károly Kós for Buffalo House, Budapest Zoo, 1908-1912.
Right: design by Károly Kós for Catholic church, Zebegény, 1908.

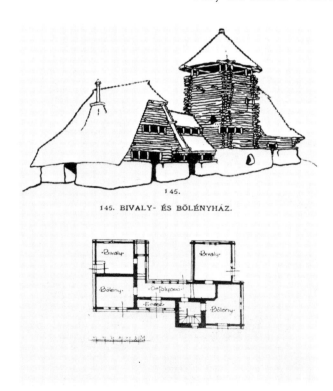

145. BIVALY- ÉS BÖLÉNYHÁZ.

was presented in a rather unsophisticated condition, and on the basis of this material they started to create a new, rustic architecture.

Like their predecessors, they obtained only a few, mostly minor commissions, among which may be mentioned the Presbyterian parsonage in Budapest-Obuda (1908–09) by Károly Kós and the church in Zebegény (1908–09) designed by Kós and Béla Jánszky. The church shows strong influences from Finland, a country which by this time was considered to have an exemplary, independent national architecture. The interior, bounded by oblique walls and day-lit from above, has a Byzantine/Romanesque mood – intensified through wall paintings by the leading painters of the Hungarian 'Pre-Raphaelites'. These 'Young Ones', admirers of John Ruskin, preached a return to the Middle Ages, since they rightly felt that the cataclysms in Magyar history prevented styles later than Gothic from being assimilated into popular art. This tendency is illustrated by buildings designed from 1908 to 1912 by Kós and Zrumeczky in the Budapest Zoo, first of all the houses for birds, for pheasants, for elks and the house (regrettably demolished) for buffaloes. It is interesting, too, to see buildings designed for animals from another continent, e.g. for ostriches, which strive to evoke the architecture of that continent.

Yet, the Obuda parsonage, besides Gothic influences, also shows the influence of the English house. This influence is demonstrable in the picturesque massing and functionality of these architects' buildings and, of course, in their magazine *A Ház* (The House) which was published for four years. Their models in this respect are M.H. Baillie Scott and C.R. Ashbee.★ All these are apparent in the Budapest schools designed by Károly Kós and Dénes Györgyi in Városmajor street (1910–11) and in that by Dezső Zrumeczky in Aldás Street (1912). Buildings located, quite deliberately, in green belts, on the Buda hills, exhibit further features of the group's activity, e.g. the frequent application of exposed timber structures wherever possible, carving in conformity with folk art traditions, simplicity of façades, strictly functional application of ornament and a creative integration of all the decorative arts.

During its brief existence, the group met with two kinds of difficulty. The many interpretations which could be put on the idea of 'national character' led to confusion: concepts such as race, people, nation, even 'Hungarian' were variously understood or misunderstood. Moreover, the realisation of their ideas was still more hampered in a concrete sense, by the inherent contradiction of matching contemporary building materials and structures with elements of popular architecture, and this forever forced compromises – particularly in the

★Some young Hungarians also worked with Ashbee, who made some objects for Hungarians and worked on a project for a house in Budapest.

Project for a house in Budapest by C.R. Ashbee, published in *Magyar Iparmüveszet*, vol. XIII, 1910, p.69.

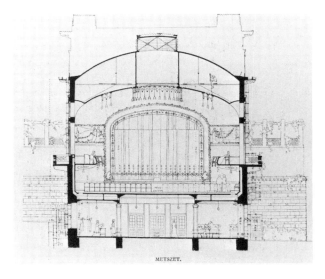

Theatre by István Medgyaszay in Veszprém, 1908. *Above:* section of auditorium. *Right:* detail showing consoles.

design of public buildings. But in spite of all this, the group still had real success both in promoting progressive architectural design, mainly based on functional requirements and rational structure, and in their search for a popular national architecture. They therefore played a crucial part in the development of the next phase of Hungarian architecture – the work of Béla Lajta and István Medgyaszay.

Both these designers insisted that modern architecture must find its point of departure in contemporary materials and structures. Both joined the movement of 'The Young Ones'. Medgyaszay, a student of François Hennebique, approached architecture from the side of reinforced concrete and, while wrestling with the transformation of popular wood carvings into concrete, he was also greatly concerned with stress patterns in reinforced concrete structures. His theatres in Veszprém (1908) and Sopron (1909), studio villas for leaders of the Hungarian Pre-Raphaelites in Godollo (1904 to 1906) and the church in Rárosmulyad (1910) clearly reflect these endeavours.

Béla Lajta followed a more conventional path. He became thoroughly acquainted with contemporary architectural concepts and works during his study-tour across half of Europe (in London, for instance, he worked in Norman Shaw's studio and learned about the work of Baillie Scott), returning home in 1900 to join Ödön Lechner. The first stage of his activity (up to 1904, which he himself called the Lechner period) does not differ much from those of Lechner's direct followers, e.g. on the Schmidl family vault, the Szirmai palace (1901, now destroyed) and the fire station at Zenta (1902).

The next stage in his activity is close in spirit to the movement of 'The Young Ones', although he was not a full member of this group and, unlike them, was never a popular architect. His works include a villa for Desző Malonyai (1908), author and editor of a book in several volumes on Hungarian folk art★, an Asylum for the Blind (1905-80) and an Almshouse in Budapest (1908-11).

The Malonyai villa is one of the most English buildings in Hungarian architecture of that period, primarily on account of its interior and furniture. At the same time, there are again traces of Finnish architecture. In general, Finnish references are quite consciously made in the Hungarian architecture of the time, since (apart from a common, if distant, ethnic origin) the use of timber and the general organic character of Finnish architecture is similar to that of Transylvanian popular architecture, bearing clear national-political aspirations, and also partly inspired by British movements.

The endeavours of 'The Young Ones' are best seen in the Asylum for the Blind, while the Almshouse may seem a rather weak link in the development of Lajta's architecture. But this only appears to be so. The building is an experiment, just like Lechner's work in the period from the Thonet House to the

Rózsavölgyi house, by Béla
Lajta, Budapest, 1911-12.

*Ilona Rév, *Épitészet és enteriőr a
magyar századfordulón*
(Architecture and Interiors in
Hungary at the Turn of the
Century), Gondolat, Budapest,
1983.

*Ferenc Merényi, *Hungarian
Architecture 1867-1967*, Műszaki,
Budapest, 1969, p.59.

Museum of Applied Arts. Lajta considered the Almshouse as an opportunity
to test his newly acquired knowledge of ornaments and materials.

About 1910, he obtained three commissions, 'the solution of which induced
him to detach himself from the earlier orientation of Hungarian architecture –
historicism, decorativism, popular and national romanticism – and to follow a
new engineering way of architecture, keeping the requirements of the job in
view, applying the latest architectural methods, while also facing up to their
aesthetic consequences.'* These three buildings – a school in Vas Street, Budapest
(1910 to 1913), the Erzsénetváros Savings Bank (1911-12) and the Rózsavölgyi
house (1911-12) – place him beside Adolf Loos, Louis Sullivan and maybe
Charles Rennie Mackintosh. Where his earlier buildings had been in garden
suburbs, these three houses were in urban settings. Possibilities were strictly
confined by the plots, as had been the case with Lechner's Post Office Savings
Bank. The circumstances on each of the three sites were rather similar; nevertheless, Latja created three different buildings, making the best use of what
amounted to little more than subtle shades of difference between situations and
commissions.

The façade, interior arrangement and decorative scheme of the school in Vas
Street are entirely of their time. The building, with an L-shaped plan but only
one façade to the street, is a set of rooms organised by two staircase cores. In
effect, the plan solution produced an original building facade. 'The composition of the building's mass, with two lateral projections of different sizes'
comprising the staircases, 'with prominent brick pilasters spanning between
storeys, is an extremely daring, masterful design . . . able to express functional
distinctions even in a narrow street of bleak blocks of flats.'* Out of the three

*Artur Bárdos, 'Béla Lajta' *in* Művészet* (Art), 1913, pp.285-294.

simultaneous projects, this one has the most compact façade and the heaviest mass. So the importance of ornament is here at its greatest. At this stage in his work, 'the Hungarian aspect as a main goal was replaced by that of meeting needs as simply and as constructively as possible and of decorating by means of the construction itself; yet Lechner's influence is still vivid in the ornament of buildings by Lajta.'* He kept all he could use from his master's ornament: the creative application of popular motifs, the enhancement of the structure with ornament, and the harmonious use of materials. Utilising the features of stone on the school façade, both entrances were emphasised with low ornaments and the building's entablature incorporated pecularities of fired clay. In the interior, everything was designed with the utmost care, from special class-rooms, laboratories and reading rooms to benches, teachers' desks, handrails and switchboards.

The other two buildings are the first internationally acceptable solutions in Hungary to a totally new problem, that of integrating a business and a residential building. Both are openly divided according to function, both are manifestly tectonic in construction, both are struggling with the problem of confining superimposed, equal storeys of similar functions. Both thus arrive at the same compromise, but, abjuring the possibility of a confined storey of service installations, as adopted by Sullivan, the crown is replaced by setting back the top storey and placing a balcony in front of it. On the Erzsébetváros Savings Bank building, which has rather homogeneous façade claddings and uniform ornamental facings between windows, there is no sharp distinction between the vertical divisions of the office section and the horizontal ones of the living storeys. But the Rózsavölgyi house disrupted its environment. The white glazed tile cladding of the living storeys, red majolica stripes instead of cornices, the appearance on the façade of the balcony crowning the building, and the conventionalised folk art motifs imitating those by Lechner – all these together were enough to put the fat on the fire. The amazingly daring structural quality of the lower, business storeys – rows of thin, plain columns and extensive areas of glass – contributed to the building's publicity value.

Lajta built some further houses and won some prizes in competitions. But World War I and a debilitating illness interrupted his career. Nevertheless, his activity raised Hungarian architecture to world level. Like the contemporaries I have mentioned above – as well as Peter Behrens, H.C. Van de Velde and others – Béla Lajta anticipated the architecture of the decades to follow.

The direct influence of Mackintosh is little felt in Hungarian art at the turn of the century. Certainly the principles of Ruskin and William Morris, works by C.F.A. Voysey, Baillie Scott, Ashbee and the Guilds were known. What reached Hungary came primarily through the great applied arts exhibitions and, of course, via Vienna. Hungarians were undoubtedly aware of Scottish national ambitions. For example, in a 1910 conference, Károly Kós, the theoretical leader of the 'The Young Ones' still felt able to assign James Macpherson and the Ossianic poems a leading place in national literary traditions, and referred to the role played by Scottish castles and mansions in British architectural traditions.* There is a more general affinity. Mackintosh, like Lechner, is a unique designer: interiors by Mackintosh and buildings by Lechner have in common two-dimensional, symbolic ornament, increasingly subordinated to function and structure. The respect and preference of Mackintosh for the Gothic is also somewhat analogous to the ideas of the 'The Young Ones'. Indeed, it is possible to draw a real comparison with the activity of Béla Lajta, for the two have in common a strongly cubic construction, a lack of cornices which results in neat outlines and a confined architectonic effect. One concrete similarity is their evident opposition to stereotyped school buildings, as for example is clear in their respective designs for the Scotland Street and Vas Street schools. The two stair turrets in Glasgow, and the two projections in Budapest hint at a close similarity of architectural concept.

*Károly Kós, 'Nemzeti Művészet' (National Art) in *Magyar Iparművészet* (Hungarian Applied Arts), 1910, pp.141-157.

Last but not least, both movements have in common a striving to create a new national character in the art of their respective countries, but a character which was both national and international.

HECTOR GUIMARD AND THE INTERNATIONAL ART NOUVEAU MOVEMENT
Claude Frontisi

Specificity and Contradictions

The desire to break with tradition emerged into the artistic consciousness only at the extreme end of the nineteenth century, becoming little by little a pressing compulsion, indeed the order of things. Until then, all that had mattered was respect for the institutions and the lessons of the Masters. In the early 1880s, Edouard Manet's only aspiration was to be accepted and recognised, and he was not a man suspected of nonconformity. Similarly, the Impressionists, in not deliberately arousing the hostility of their fellow painters, the peevishness of the press or the indifference of the public, became marginal, at least for a time.

On the other hand, for an artist like Paul Gauguin (whose links with Art Nouveau are clear), the break with tradition arose from a truly 'inner necessity'. So that he could free himself from the prestigious and unrelenting burden of Western tradition, his sole purpose was to achieve a physical and mental break with European culture, history, institutions and, above all, visual imagery.

The Art Nouveau movement was the first to proclaim a general desire for a fresh start and as such anticipated the avant-garde movements, like the Italian Futurists, who rejected Art Nouveau with violence. Sometimes it even engendered new movements; the Bauhaus, for example, was its successor in more ways than one. The idea of break is further borne out by the terminology used: Art Nouveau, Modern Style, Jugendstil and Secession are all titles used by leading practitioners themselves and not pejorative epithets imposed by way of criticism or handed down by tradition, as was the case for Impressionism and Cubism.

This view should be sufficient to permit a full re-evaluation of Art Nouveau and to reintroduce it into the general perspective of art history, cleansed of all suspicion of kitsch, retromania and other subjects of speculation. As the inaugural phase of twentieth-century art, its main feature was its compliance, even to excess, with the demands of modernity. Hector Guimard was both the herald and the impetuous defender of this idea, for it was he who, in order to describe the architectural style of which he was the promoter in France, used the title '*Art Moderne*'.

Formative Period

Hector Guimard was born in Lyon in 1867 – the year of the death of Jean-Auguste-Dominique Ingres. One can always find something symbolic in a coincidence like this. The painter, it is said not without ambiguity, was the originator and the incarnation of academic absolutism in the nineteenth century, and it is precisely against that institution that Guimard set himself. The ambiguous and contradictory manner in which he did this sheds light on the relatively short reign of the 'pontiff' of Art Nouveau as well as on that of the movement as a whole.

From its beginnings, the architect's career seems to have been determined by a number of precocious yet convergent decisions, which, with the benefit of hindsight, seem remarkable in such a young man who came from a provincial background without any recognisable artistic leaning.

He was fifteen years old when he arrived in Paris and entered the Ecole des Arts Décoratifs. The importance of this first orientation cannot be too strongly emphasised. He was straight away confronted by the applied arts/fine arts dilemma, from which Art Nouveau, as one of its essential characteristics, was to propose a way out. In a similar vein, the naturalist option of Gustave Raulin, in particular the study of vegetal and floral decoration, appears as fundamental, being far removed from academic models, historicism and treatises.

Guimard was to attract attention and in 1891 would return to his school to teach drawing – as Eugène-Emmanuel Viollet-le-Duc had done before him.

In 1885, having got his diploma, his second move was to enter the Ecole des Beaux Arts. It was undoubtedly in the 'free studio' of Charles Genys, heir to the Viollet-le-Duc tradition, that Guimard became familiar with the design philosophy handed down by the author of *Conversations on Architecture*: rejection of servile imitation; faithful expression of materials, of function and, therefore, of form; the pluralist practice of the art of designing and building; a taste for new technologies. Having fully absorbed these lessons, Guimard was to acknowledge Viollet-le-Duc in his later declarations. He was to go one better in 1895 in his use of 'V' supports for his Ecole du Sacré-Coeur, and thus render 'true homage' to him, by making a reality of the 'keel of cast iron columns' project illustrated in chapter XII of *Conversations*.

The third decisive factor was Guimard's joining the Société Nationale des Beaux Arts. This society had been founded in 1890 as the result of a split in the heart of the all-powerful and official Society of French Artists. This divorce can be understood as much through the conflicts between individuals as it was by the legitimate reactions of young 'tearaways' who were impatient to shake off the shackles of artistic conformism. (Jean-Louis-Ernest Meissonnier belonged to the 'rebel' group and died the year after its foundation.) Whatever it may have been, it was soon described in other countries as the 'French Secession'. Guimard, who had been admitted to the Artistes Français in 1890, joined the dissident society in 1894, and there came across Anatole de Baudot again, the principal successor to Viollet-le-Duc. This was the first of a long series of spectacular and non-conformist actions by the young architect.

The support of Anatole de Baudot and the success of his first buildings resulted in Guimard being awarded a travelling scholarship. In the minds of its promoters, this must have been as a modest substitute for the Grand Prix de Rome (which Guimard had turned down) and enabled the winner to make a trip and have a period of study abroad.

Ecole du Sacré-Coeur, Paris 16ème, 1895. Detail of façade.

Castel Béranger, Paris 16ème, 1896-98.

It was indubitably implicit that this should take place in Italy, the universal land of the arts. However, Guimard chose to go to England. He went there on two occasions – in the summers of 1894 and 1895. The sketches that he left show clearly how he nourished his appetite for the picturesque in architecture, for cottages, and it was here that he adopted the bow-window. In a quick note, he mentions having gone to Scotland, but, alas, not the slightest description of this trip is to be found.

In 1895, on his way home via Holland and Belgium, Guimard met Victor Horta, his elder by a few years, whom he considered for a time as his master. A short but significant meeting: Guimard discovered the Hôtel Tassel. He returned to Paris wholly won over to Art Nouveau and took on the rôle of proclaimer of Horta's dictum: 'It is not the flower that I like to take as a decorative element, but its stem.'

Guimard immediately put it into practice in his Castel Béranger, which was then under construction. This building obtained fairly wide approval, some praise and even an official award. Nonetheless, its style also provoked violent attacks and, because of its origins, the unleashing of unimaginable xenophobia.

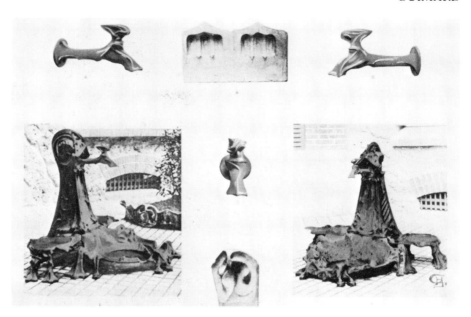

Castel Béranger. The fountain.

Soon all the ambiguity that comes with success manifested itself and the definitive break between Guimard and the upholders of official architecture finally took place. The events which marked the start of his career and the choices made by Guimard during these years make it quite clear that he did nothing to try to prevent such a divorce.

Development

Art Nouveau is diversity itself. At its beginning, a multiplicity of component parts can be found: the vernacular, orientalism, the industrial arts, the cult of the line, etc. It would also be pointless to attempt to box into a narrow typology the existence of such strongly differing individualists as Antoni Gaudí, Charles Rennie Mackintosh or Guimard, all of whom developed in different ways. Guimard's development falls into five principal, fairly distinct phases.

During the first (1888-95), Guimard's output was essentially made up of small private houses built in the west of Paris, or more precisely in Auteuil, which had recently become part of the City of Paris. Their form is derived from 'picturesque architecture' with, as fidelity to Viollet-le-Duc demanded, numerous borrowings from the medieval repertory. Guimard interpreted the latter in two ways, between which he hesitated – one severe and Romanesque (Hôtel Delfau in Rue Molitor), and the other Gothic, where he indulged in its lyrical vein (Hôtel Jassède in Rue Chardon-Lagache). What makes his work distinctive is his strong taste for a very lively interplay of projections and recesses.

Among the materials that he used in a rationalist manner, brick played an essential role, as much for economic reasons as for the decorative use of its varied textures and colourings – a polychromy reinforced by the occasional use of ceramics. From this time, Guimard's activities encompassed the entire art of building: ironwork, stained glass, decorative elements and furniture. In this the personality of Viollet-le-Duc asserts itself and, in germ, one of the fundamental characteristics of all Art Nouveau.

The second stage, a crucial one, concerns his introduction to Art Nouveau, described previously. It was extremely short, for Guimard succeeded in the course of two years in adapting himself to the new manner and in creating a whole repertory of forms that were both typical of the movement yet belonged to no-one but him – something that can hardly be said of a multiplicity of imitators and parodists. Castel Béranger, with its neo-Gothic framework, was the melting pot in which this change took place. When it was finished in 1898, Guimard was identified not just with this work, of which he was the creator right down to the smallest detail, but with Art Nouveau as a whole, which had come to be known in France as the 'Style Guimard'.

Castel Henriette, Sèvres, 1899–1900 (destroyed 1969) in a postcard, 'Le Style Guimard'.

Maison Coilliot, Lille, 1898–1900. Shop sign.

Salle Humbert de Romans, Paris 16ème, 1898-1900 (destroyed around 1908). Section.

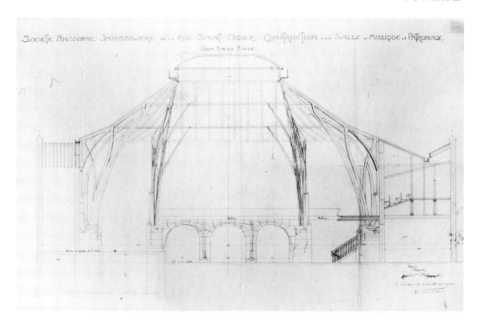

La Hublotière, Hermanville, c.1900. Detail of half-timbering.

After this exemplary venture, Guimard was, until about 1905, at the height of his career, and it appeared, at least to begin with, that Art Nouveau had won some credibility in France. This was a fruitful period, with works as diverse and original as the Castel Henriette at Sèvres (destroyed in 1969), the Maison Coilliot in Lille, La Bluette and La Surprise (destroyed 1942), both on the Channel coast, the Castel d'Orgeval to the south of Paris and, in the capital itself, the Salle Humbert de Romans (destroyed around 1908), the Hôtel Nozal (destroyed in 1957) and the apartment building in the Avenue de Versailles, to mention only the most notable examples.

It was from the entrances and the stations of the Paris Métro (the latter have all disappeared) which are so typical of the style, that Art Nouveau got one of its nicknames: the *style Métro*. During this period, production of furniture and decorative elements increased and became more diverse.

Castel d'Orgeval, Villemoisson, 1905, from the side.

In 1903, the Paris Exhibition of Building took place. Guimard was to some degree its hero: he gave a lecture in the Grand Palais, received an award and had a series of retrospective postcards of his work printed which he named without the slightest modesty, 'Le Style Guimard'. But all this was something of a pyrrhic victory: the press, almost as a body, came out against Guimard and against Art Nouveau as a whole which, it has to be said, was in the process of sinking or wandering into the worst aberrations of what was called the 'Noodle Style'. Commissions became rarer. Perhaps Guimard himself sobered down a bit. One can see confirmation of this in the difference between the design for

Hôtel Guimard, Paris 16ème, 1909, side elevation.

the Hôtel Deron-Levant (1905), which was still very exuberant, and its real-isation in 1908, which was much calmer, close even to a certain Classicism. It was thus that Guimard set off on another stage of his career, with a repertory of forms that was much more restrained, more repetitive, yet with his own stylistic mannerisms. His own house in Avenue Mozart, the Hôtel Mezzara in Rue la Fontaine and the Synagogue in Rue Pavée all have a refined elegance and were impressive successes. For the time being, until the start of World War I, Guimard remained on the path of Art Nouveau, even though he was the only person following it.

In 1914, Guimard abruptly changed his repertory for an office building – he abandoned the curve for the angular forms of regular cross-members and the verticals of bow windows in a style that, early though it was, can be identified as Art Deco.

After the war, he built nothing but apartment buildings, in the same formal language, to which he gave, as we might expect, his own personalised inter-pretation, with here and there some decorative reminders of his past manner.

Up to 1914, Guimard's architecture contained the characteristics that one would expect to find in Art Nouveau:

— asymmetry

— the dominance of line

— in the debate over the flower and the stem, Guimard settled in favour of the latter, both as a decorative element and as a dynamic principle

— ornament was structural, and in certain cases, functional (he formed the mould for a door handle by simply squeezing a lump of clay in his hand)

— lastly, he achieved the ideal of being both master of works and total artist, tackling all fields related to architecture: artistic cast iron for balconies, ironwork, stained glass, ceramics and mosaic, carpets and hangings, wall-paper, ironmongery for building and furnishing, furniture, ornaments and lettering.

But Guimard would not be a true representative of the movement had he not been a strong individualist. He was no theorist. His philosophy was con-tained in three words set out when he was working on the Castel Béranger: Logic, Feeling, Harmony. He stuck to this rather unclear formula all through his career. He had no pupils and few known followers.

Throughout his life's work, Guimard's concepts remained impregnated with rationalism. To be persuaded of this, one has only to compare his country house at Vanves dated 1893 and La Guimardière, which Guimard built for himself in 1930: same function, same structure.

In every case, it is noticeable that he took great care to adapt to each site and to the local vernacular. In the case of La Bluette, Guimard adopted Norman half timbering and the walls were built with large pebbles and shells.

The way in which he managed to make the most out of awkward and tiny building plots was remarkable. In the Rue Greuze, he built an apartment building of eight storeys on a site which was no more than four or five metres in depth, even using bow-windows for the kitchens and bathrooms!

Guimard was constantly attracted to the abstract for his decorative and or-namental forms, and, particularly at the time of the Castel Béranger, to the strange and the fantastic – though never quite to the same degree as Gaudí. These forms owed their essence in each case to a sharp awareness of the texture of the materials used.

One cannot but be struck by the large number of Guimard's works that have suffered destruction. This, the ultimate trait of so many Art Nouveau buildings, is worthy of note. They became choice targets, abandoned to the property speculators through public indifference. Thus the Maison du Peuple suffered the same fate as the Salle Humbert de Romans and Castel Henriette a similar one to that of the Hôtel Aubecq. Guimard and Horta, without doubt, would never have dreamt that their work would suffer such a convergent fate.

Hôtel Mezzara, Paris 16ème, 1909.

Guimard the Innovator

Hector Guimard was not just a fertile creator or, as he put it, an 'Architect of Art'. 'Architecture is not designed, it is built,' he wrote in a letter to Horta. In fact, he was an accomplished building technician, a pioneer and sometimes an inventor of modern solutions.

A man of the century of the industrial revolutions, he became a skilled user of metal. His first works were contemporary with the Exposition Universelle of 1889, in which iron emerged triumphant in the Eiffel Tower and the Salle des Machines. He rapidly mastered its potential: his Ecole du Sacré-Coeur (1895) is built entirely as an overhang, the principal façade and the edge of the first floor sitting on a monumental metallic edge beam which is no less decorative than the pillars which support it.

Next, the notion of serial production began to occupy Guimard's thinking, no doubt from the time of Castel Béranger and effectively from 1900. One should not ignore the fact that the surrounds of the Metro entrances allow a flexibility for any form of opening and that repetition, pure and simple, is only apparent. The modular moulds of 'artistic cast ironwork' published in 1907 were actually used from 1900 onwards. They were produced industrially and examples of them can be found in various places in France. Finally, pushing logic to its extreme, Guimard developed the idea of serial production into that of prefabrication. In 1920 he registered a series of copyrights for houses with standardised and prefabricated elements which could be assembled without either a qualified workforce or a measuring instrument. The success of the one built example makes it regrettable that the idea passed unnoticed. The process of supporting ceiling panels in the lower flange of metal floor joists, in use around 1896, again provided a solution that is both economical and aesthetically pleasing. Also at the Castel Béranger, one of the very first examples of walls of coloured glass brick is to be found.

Guimard was no doubt tempted by reinforced concrete from as early as 1896 (Hennebique's patents date from 1892). Nevertheless he resisted it until 1928, when he used it for his last Paris apartment building, employing the system developed by his friend, Henri Sauvage.

In a period when he foresaw technological and economic change and pioneered some of its processes and its new materials, he limited himself to a type of production – that of the artist-craftsman – which was to become increasingly unsuitable and to be doomed by the demands of high output.

It should perhaps be mentioned how different he was from Henri Sauvage, with whom he was very close. Sauvage built public housing and dreamed of the city of the future. No trace can be found in Guimard's work of such views of the future, except perhaps in an extra-architectural and utopian project for a world organisation of nations to prevent further armed conflict. After the rejection of Art Nouveau, Guimard pursued a career as an architect/decorator – more an artist-craftsman than a pioneer of design.

Thus Guimard, in his own way, lived out the contradictions of Art Nouveau. An ardent apostle of stylistic renewal during the cubist period, he remained faithful to an art for which decoration was essential at the precise moment when a formal and radical movement endeavoured to reject it.

Guimard, who had been accused of architectural anarchy, remained hemmed into a geographically and sociologically tight-knit circle of traditionalist clients – it is astonishing that they accepted, for a while, his fundamental nonconformity and even took a delight in it. Then, faced with general hostility from the institutions, from his fellow architects and the public, all Guimard could do was allow himself to be shut into this gilded isolation – forced to live out in a bourgeois manner a period that was crucial from all points of view.

Such are the paradoxes of Guimard, a man whose work found an essential link in the history of architecture and decoration, sandwiched between the Exposition Universelle of 1889 and the Bauhaus. In conclusion, one further paradox is perhaps worthy of mention: condemned for unyielding individuality, the work of Guimard and of the Art Nouveau movement in general have been revived for precisely that reason, so much has the captivating charm of their strangeness become indispensable to us today.

THE PERSONALITY OF ANTONI GAUDÍ

Juan Bassegoda Nonell

[1] J.F. Ràfols Fontanals, *Gaudí*, Ed. Canosa, Barcelona, 1929

[2] The first named is author of several books on Gaudí, outstanding of which is: C. Martinell, *Gaudí, su vida, su teoria, su obra*, Official Association of Architects of Catalonia and the Balearic Islands, Barcelona, 1967.

Isidro Puig Boada wrote in 1929 *El Templo de la Sagrada Familia* which has been published four times, the last time in 1982 in Spanish.

Francisco Folguera wrote the second, critical part of the 1929 book by Ràfols.

[3] Juan Bergós Massó, *Gaudí, l'home i l'obra*, Ed. Ariel, Barcelona, 1953. Spanish version by Olga de los Rios, Barcelona Polytechnic University Publishing House, 1974.

George R. Collins, Antonio Gaudí, Braziller, New York, 1960. Spanish version, Ed. Bruguera, 1961. Other editions in German and French.

Juan Matamala Flotats, *Gaudí, mi itinerario con el arquitecto*, 1960 (unpublished).

Roberto Pane, *Gaudí*, Ed. di Communità, Milan, 1964

Juan Bassegoda *et al*, *The complete works of Gaudí*, Rikkuyo-Sha Publishing Co. Ltd. Tokyo, 1978 (in Japanese)

Antoni Gaudí i Cornet (1852-1926) has been studied primarily through his architectural and artistic work. However, at the same time as writing about his buildings, various authors have made honest attempts to write his biography.

They have run up against enormous difficulties in both tasks. Gaudí's architecture is unlike any other and it is extremely difficult for the writer to find parallels or antecedents. On the other hand, there is very little written on Gaudí's life, since he never showed the slightest interest in divulging his intimate feelings.

Gaudí became famous whilst still very young, but his biography was not written until after his death. This was by J.F. Ràfols,[1] who published his book in 1929, although he collected many of the details while the master was still alive, when he worked as draughtsman in the workshop of the Templo Expiatorio de la Sagrada Familia. Other architects such as C. Martinell, Isidro Puig Boada and Francisco Folguera[2] knew Gaudí during his life, but their biographical or critical texts date from after 1929, except for short journalistic articles. The great studies on Gaudí, except for Ràfols's valuable document, appeared only after the 1952 centenary of Gaudí's birth. Among these are works by Juan Bergós (1953), George R. Collins (1960), Juan Matamala (also 1960), Roberto Pane (1964), Martinell (1967) and Bassegoda (1978).[3]

Those who knew Gaudí personally described an already elderly man, enthusiastic for his work on the Sagrada Familia but deeply distressed by a number of events which had affected him considerably from 1912.

Tortoise at the base of the column on the north side of the doorway in the Nativity façade of the Sagrada Familia. Since ancient times, the tortoise has represented the idea of a sphere and has thus been a symbol of the cosmos emerging from chaos. As the chaos disappeared, the cosmos had to be fixed to the earth by the cardinal points, symbolised by the four feet of the tortoise. Above the ordered sphere of the cosmos rises the column that supports the church, symbol of the ultimate order.

Portico of the crypt of the Colonia Güell at Santa Coloma de Cervelló. The vaults are hyperbolic paraboloids which for Gaudí symbolised the Holy Trinity, with Father and Son as the directrices and the Holy Ghost as the generatrix.

★On the personality and work of Francisco Berenguer, see the doctoral thesis of the architect José Luis Ros Pérez, *Los dibujos de un modernista*', 1983 (unpublished).

★Gaudí designed a monument (which was never built) in honour of this Bishop in front of the Passion façade of the Sagrada Familia.

★P. Miquel d'Esplugues, O.M.C., *El primer comte de Güell*, Barcelona, 1921

In that year, his orphaned niece Rosa Egea, who lived at his home in the Park Güell, died. His faithful collaborator Francisco Berenguer Mestres★ also died, and in 1914 Gaudí was involved in a lawsuit with the Milà family for questions of professional fees due for the Casa Milà project; in 1915, there was a serious financial crisis affecting the Sagrada Familia which almost caused the cessation of works; in 1916, his friend the Bishop of Vic, Dr. Torras i Bages★, died; in 1917 the works on the Church at the Güell colony in Santa Coloma de Cervelló were finally interrupted, and his friend and patron Eusebio Güell Bacigalupi★ died in 1918.

Authors such as Collins, Pane or Bassegoda never knew Gaudí and could therefore only carry out their biographical research indirectly through documents.

Obviously between 1878, the year in which he graduated from his university career, and 1912, the year in which the series of misfortunes began, Gaudí the architect must have been a very different person from the Gaudí known by his disciples and subsequent biographers and from the young student Gaudí and the child and adolescent Gaudí of whom only slender, confusing references are available.

★The donation of the architect Domingo Sugranes Gras, who continued Gaudí's work on the Sagrada Familia.

★J. Bassegoda, *El único articulo de Gaudí*, Miscellania Barcinonensia, Barcelona, June 1976.

★Eufemià Fort i Cogul, *Gaudí i la restauració de Poblet, Episodis de la Història 208,* Rafael Dalmau, Barcelona, 1976

★Files of the Museum of the Caminos. Astorga.

★Joan Maragall, *Una Calaverada*, Illustració Catalana, 2nd year, No 20, Barcelona, November 1904

Work in progress on the crypt of the Sagrada Familia in 1889. Only the chapel of San José had been completed; it had been consecrated on 19th March 1885. Behind is Gaudí's office, built in 1887.

Gaudí's thoughts are known only through his architectural works or through the sayings picked up devotedly by his admirers from 1915 onwards. He wrote very little and what he did scarcely clarifies his personality, although all of it dates from his youth. It is made up of his diary as a student (now in the Reus Museum★), a single article published in *La Renaixença* in 1881 and the memorandum on his lamp-post project for the streets of Barcelona in 1878.★ The so-called manuscript of Poblet, dating from 1870, was written only by Eduardo Toda in spite of having been repeatedly attributed to Toda, Gaudí and Ribera★.

The manuscript or diary of Reus also contains a specification for the construction of Gaudí's own writing desk (1878) and comments on the Christian temple and on the family seat which may well have been simple notes taken in a class at the School of Architecture, as Collins thinks, as well as a text on ornamentation which is the most interesting.

Thus there are some writings dating from between 1876 and 1881 and some sayings collected by his disciples and followers between 1915 and 1926. There is, therefore, an enormous gap devoid of information between 1881 and the time when Gaudí shut himself up in the Sagrada Familia. All that remains is his laconic but biting letter of resignation as Director of the Works of the Episcopal Palace of Astorga in 1893★.

Ràfols had the opportunity of seeing Gaudí's documents at his home in Park Güell shortly after the master's death and mentions certain letters to friends which help very little towards a serious study. This material, like the rest of Gaudí's files, was destroyed at the Sagrada Familia in 1936 by the revolutionary hordes.

With such disparate and slender resources, any attempt to define Gaudí's personality as a man stumbles against insuperable obstacles which only the imagination of the writers can transcend by creating fictional biographies to deceive the reader. For example, there are several accounts of Gaudí's love life, which he himself never even mentioned either in writing or by word of mouth. Joan Maragall,★ although avoiding subsequent liability by not citing any names, tells the story of an enamoured architect, of his trip to France to find his loved one already married and his disconsolate return to Barcelona without even having seen her. There is no reference to any particular persons, time or place. It is a poetic story, the fruit of Maragall's imagination.

Bergós mentions three alleged girl friends of Gaudí, the same one as Maragall, one who became a nun with Gaudí's blessing and a third whom he left because he thought she was a Protestant. He does not cite any names or dates.

*According to Lluis Bonet, architect of the Sagrada Familia.

Benet Gari has followed with closer attention and full knowledge the relationship around 1884 between Gaudí and Miss Pepita Moreu of Mataró which did not prosper, as the family apparently felt that Gaudí was not good enough for their daughter.*

Gaudí remained single all his life. His family was made up of his father and his niece who lived with him in Barcelona until their respective deaths in 1906 and 1912. His mother had died in 1876, when he was still a student at the School of Architecture.

After the death of Rosa Egea, Gaudí's life became solitary and reclusive, as I was told by some nuns who cared for his house in the Park Güell.

Unrequited love in his youth and then loneliness when older could have inclined Gaudí toward misanthropy, but study of his works, both of his youth and of his maturity, reveals a creative force, a firm will and an imagination which of necessity had to be born of a person in a state of grace and not of the poor, sad devil, suggested by some caricaturist.*

*José Maria Garrut, *Gaudí en la caricatura*, San Jorge, 37. Barcelona, January 1960.

Psychological and psychoanalytical studies have attempted to find the reason for Gaudí's personality, but the lack of verifiable detail has made such studies unreliable.*

*Delfi Abella, *Retrat Caracteriològic de Gaudí*, Criterion, 23, Barcelona, 1964.

Finally, the alleged Hermetism and other subtleties have inspired the naïve with ideas of magic. One writer has guessed that Gaudí was a descendant of the Agotes* and therefore a continuer of the building techniques of the Templars and, worse yet, that he was a drug addict, who took the extract of a hallucinogenic mushroom. All of this is baseless, and merely a way of attracting attention by recourse to feigned science, to witchcraft or to people from other planets.

*Joan Llarch, *Gaudí, una biografia mágica*, Barcelona, 1982.

Gaudí, artistically loquacious, was always quiet on what he considered to be his sacred privacy, but his brilliant architecture, mingled with his silence, made him a firm candidate to be the leading character of novelistic biographies

Detail of the Nativity façade of the Sagrada Familia, with representations of farmyard fowl, flowers and vegetables as well as scenes of the Flight into Egypt and the Massacre of the Innocents.

which, mistakenly representing apparently strange facts of his life, thread together a whole string of senseless consequences which reach as far as tarot, the Alexandrian cabbala or alchemy. There are works of this type which are pure fable, of interest only for the mass consumer, with a magic Gaudí, as magic sells well, much better than serious research based on certain, proven facts.

There are other writers who, in good faith, have been surprised to see that some facts of the master's life and certain sayings of his appear to coincide with expressions of the Hermetic language of alchemy. Such is the case with the study by Fernández de Castro that contains an analysis of certain of Gaudí's sayings and even of Gaudinian scholars which appear to be related to the cryptic expressions of the alchemists.

It is curious how Fernández de Castro goes so far as to find a Hermetic sense in statements extracted from books of the present writer, who has never felt any affection for alchemy.

Of all Gaudí's sayings which have been assigned some esoteric sense, there is one which is especially meaningful:

'On the Nativity façade of the Sagrada Familia, there is something for everyone. The farmers see the chickens and ducks that remind them of their farms, the scientists identify the signs of the zodiac, the geneaologists discover the genealogy of Jesus, but the explanation, the reasoning, is only known by those who are competent and should not be disclosed.'★

★The sayings of Gaudí reproduced in this paper were collected by Juan Bergós in 1919 and were published in Spanish translation in Hogar y Arquitectura, Madrid, V-VI, 1974.

Fernández de Castro comments on these statements, saying that the works of the master speak, albeit in an obscure language, like Gaudí himself, and that this saying, although capable of other interpretations, if studied from the perspective of alchemy, leads in one direction: to give sense to what for the majority is a strange life. This is putting the cart before the horse, by starting from the language of the alchemists and to seeing to what extent it coincides with what Gaudí said.

The saying may be understood more simply. The Nativity façade is architecture, and making architecture means combining an ensemble of different things and obtaining unity with all of them.

In his architecture, Gaudí uses natural decorative elements like the representation of the hens, ducks or doves, as well as countless examples of plants. He has recourse to the signs of the zodiac to set exactly the position of the stars at the coming of Christ and explains the genealogy of Christ with human figures.

Therefore, farmers, scientists and theologians, acting only in terms of their professions, will be particularly interested in the fragments of the façade that contain elements within their specific competence. This is known as occupational idiosyncrasy. Then Gaudí says that the reasoning, the explanation is only known by those who are competent and should not be disclosed. Who are the competent ones? What is the explanation, the reasoning and why should it not be disclosed?

The competent ones will be those who are capable of assimilating the synthesis of the multiple elements of the façade, those who experience architecture as an integrating art.

1:10 plaster model of the interior of the naves of the Sagrada Familia. The vaults, which resemble flower petals, are, geometrically speaking, hyperboloids.

The explanation, which Gaudí also calls reasoning, is that it is not a question of telling a fairy story but of describing something tied together with logic, with reason. It is the synthesis which forms the purpose of architecture, combining and appealing to other arts and sciences to create the unity which is the perfect, complete building.'

Clarification is to be found in another saying by Gaudí. 'Wisdom is superior to science, it comes from *sapere*, or to savour, it refers to the concrete fact.' It is synthesis, a synthesis which is very hard to attain since, Gaudí adds, 'man's intelligence acts only in two dimensions whereas that of the angels acts in three. Man may not act there until he has seen the fact, the implementation'.

This means that the implementation, the architectural fact, which is three-dimensional, is only attained on rare occasions, since not every building is a work of art, a work of wisdom, a work which may be savoured, which makes you vibrate with aesthetic emotion.

Wire mesh models for the angels descending the columns of the lateral naves of the Sagrada Familia.

It seems logical that the explanation, the reasoning, is not disclosed, not because it is mysterious of itself or because its disclosure is sinful, but because only the wise, those who can understand the architect's work of synthesis, are capable of savouring the result. It should not therefore be disclosed because nobody would get anything out of knowing it unless he were competent, wise, capable of seeing the beauty and feeling emotion with it, of savouring it.

The consideration, then, is a practical one, as it is imprudent to waste time explaining something to somebody who cannot understand it.

According to Gaudí, the angels always understand him because of their three-dimensional intelligence, but among men only a few, the most equipped with sensitivity, manage to see it, albeit fragmentarily.

Many people speak, write and publish on art. The history of art is made and composed. Styles, periods, crises, artists' lives are explained, but art, which in its highest expression is contained in very few works, is only exceptionally understood by man. It is like a flash, a momentary ray of light which briefly allows the understanding of all the beauty that man is capable of producing in certain states of angelic inspiration.

All of this, nevertheless, has nothing to do with alchemy, the inveterate obstinacy of these who stir the sulphur in the mortar in the vain hope of obtaining the gold of the philosopher's stone. If alchemy is understood as the alchemist's way of perfection in search of the glister, not of gold, but of truth, that is another story. Alchemy as a symbol would then be the equivalent of a life of internal improvement of the sort proposed by all religions, but such a path is a matter of spiritual work and not the task of the melting pot, sulphur and mortar.

Among Gaudí's sayings are pointers to the need to follow this line: 'Life is a struggle, strength is needed, and strength is a virtue which is only sustained and increased with the cultivation of the spirit, with the practice of religion.' At another time, he said to Bergós: 'Everybody makes mistakes, but the one who makes least mistakes is the one who repeats systematically.'

The alchemist may obstinately repeat the beating of his mixtures, but constancy in work, perseverance, is an abstract, generalised virtue that is not limited only to the practice of alchemy.

Gaudí said of himself that he felt he had an intense sensitivity, but lacked the precision and the consistency of the sound knowledge, that long and painful persistence, repetition and research used by the great masters, Leonardo da Vinci and Benvenuto Cellini, which endowed their works with value. All of this must be done with pain, with torture which in the end is forgotten and leaves the work as though it were spontaneous for its simplicity. This is only attained with the greatest pains, which give value to the small troubles of life and make such trifles scatter like dry leaves from the trees before the wind. These pains are constant up to death and lead to dissatisfaction with one's own work. He who is satisfied with his work had better retire, as great works are only obtained through pain, but of this scattering of the soul, precious fragments, fruit of a savour and a perfume which satiate generations, remain.

Once again there appears the way of perfection, the breaking with the artist's own spirit who leaves behind him fragments of his spirit in the form of works of art which are fruit of excellent savour and exquisite perfume which satiates the generations to follow with pleasure.

There is contained in this saying one of the best explanations of what is deemed to be mysterious in Gaudí's work: the lack of disciples, the non-existence of a Gaudinian school.

Not all architects are prepared to suffer these pains of the spirit, which are lifelong and culminate in the traumatic fragmentation of the soul. One aspect is the inspiration, skill and technique required; a very different thing is the sustained, constant sacrifice.

Gaudí explains, through the words of his friend, the Bishop of Vic, Josep Torras i Bages (1846-1916), how mortification of the body, which generates the joy of the spirit, should be practised through continuous persistent work, bodily exercise, soberness in meals and drink, and sleep. These mortifications are

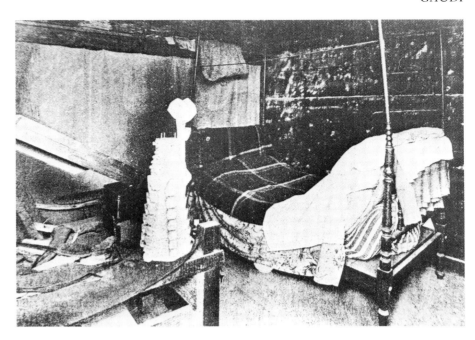

Gaudí's bed in his studio at the Sagrada Familia. Gaudí spent the last eight months of his life living in this studio in the Temple so that he could be closer to his work.

★Enric Jardí, *Història del Cercle Artístic de Sant Lluc*, Destino, Barcelona, 1976

not at all exceptional, as continuous insistent work may be a genuine pleasure, bodily exercise is no martyrdom unless it is combined with the dull idea of competition, that is when a game has to be won or a record broken, and soberness in meals does not mean constant fasting with the bread and water of fourth-century Theban anchorites, but the certainty of good digestion and the correct development of one's metabolism. In no sin is its own penitence found unless it be in unbridled gluttony. Soberness in drink, which does not mean prohibition, but the pleasure of the fine connoisseur, is health and joy, since there is nothing sadder for a man than to have an unhealthy liver or a brain attacked by alcohol. As far as moderation in sleep is concerned, sleeping just enough and getting up early guarantee a good disposition for work and a clear mind. The whole process recommended by Bishop Torras, founder with Gaudí and the Llimonas of the Artistic Circle of Sant Lluc in 1893★, prepares the spirit for the splitting apart proposed by Gaudí. It is therefore a dual way towards perfection that only a very limited number of people have the inspiration and skill to follow to the very end.

To all this Gaudí adds another truly unanswerable statement: 'Elegance is the sister of poverty, but poverty should not be confused with misery.' Poverty that is not misery is the lack of ambition, itself daughter of envy and pride; it is asceticism of spirit, not having or claiming to have as absolute needs superfluous things that only give airs and awake the envy of others. How many rich people are miserable and how many poor of spirit are full of dignity and peace of mind!

Gaudí finishes his comment on pain by saying that 'everybody has to suffer.' 'The dead,' he says, 'do not suffer. He who does not want to suffer, wants to die.'

Gaudí's clarity of thought is extraordinary and he separates one phenomenon from another with astounding discrimination. For example, he demarcates the limits of the competence of art and science. He considers 'science to be the fruit of analysis.' The process is he says, 'like the dissection of a dead body.' 'Wisdom,' which he identifies with art, 'is wealth, science serves only to keep false currency out of circulation.'

Wisdom and art lead to 'beauty which is the glow of truth and seduces every body. Science is only for intelligent people.' He finishes by saying that 'art, masculine, fecundates science which is female, science which is learned with demonstrations while art is learned with examples, the masterpieces of the past,' those which satiate generations.

To end this study of Gaudí through the sayings of his maturity, three of them may be cited which form the crowning point of his thought throughout a life devoted only to trial, to study and to the improvement of architecture.

Gaudí said that he was thinking of placing ascending figures of the blessed people and descending figures of angels in a set of two crossing spirals on the columns of the Sagrada Familia. Thus intelligences of two and three dimensions described by him are mingled together. An alchemist may see in this symbol the famous star of David with the two equilateral triangles, the symbolism of which is precisely the same. It may be a consequence or a coincidence although the difference lies in the signposting elementariness of the Jewish star and the three-dimensional beauty of the waving surfaces that are the spirals.

Another saying worth remembering is: 'Glory is light, light is joy, and joy is the pleasure of the spirit.' This means that the pleasure of the spirit is not to be found in intellectual digression, in vanguardism or in science taken over by aberrant technology, but in light, equivalent to glory, to the shining of the truth, rare and hardly seen even after years of constancy and orderly sacrifice.

Finally, the most famous of Gaudí's sayings which expresses his naïve yet deep thought in its exquisite simplicity is: 'Originality consists of returning to the origin. It should not be sought in extravagance. One should know what one regularly does and improve on it always.' A recipe which is both the statement of a wise man and a confession of humility.

In Barcelona, in Majorca, in Astorga, in León and in Comillas lie the fragments of the soul of Gaudí crushed after years of prudent mortification in search of the savoury fruit, perhaps the golden apples, the oranges from the garden of the Hesperides which he placed over the dragon at the entrance of the Güell Estate in Barcelona, bittersweet fruit that satiate the present generation which is increasingly seeing in Gaudí the incarnation of the spirit of genuine architecture: that which derives from the forms of Nature, masterpiece of the Creator and the Great Architect of the world.

Principal stairway of the Park Güell, the most naturalistic of Gaudí's works, in which the combination of ingenuity and sensuality that characterise his architecture can be seen.

MACKINTOSH FURNITURE: REASSESSMENT FOR RECONSTRUCTION

Filippo Alison

In this paper I wish to dwell on two themes which to some extent correspond with my interest in interior architecture. These are the continuing validity of Charles Rennie Mackintosh's design, as evidenced through a remarkable resurgence of appreciation of his work, and the problems connected with its reconstruction. At first, the two themes may appear unrelated, even opposed. Yet they are simply two aspects of a single reality.

Scholars are now thinking about reassessing the limited and possibly outdated critical evaluations which present Mackintosh as a forerunner of the Modern Movement, as an exponent of Art Nouveau, or as the last romantic, bound to the vernacular forms of his own cultural milieu. Such evaluations, based on scholarly principles and historical analysis, stress only parts of a much richer overall picture.

I have always given equal weight to Mackintosh's formalism, his adhesion to what in Italy we call the *stile Liberty* and his particular use of structure as a decorative element. In his work the figurative permeates the formal structure, indeed the figurative quality of the object determines its structural organisation. The real lesson to be drawn from his work lies in Mackintosh's conscious determination that modern architecture should answer a need for a more satisfying environment and should spring from a thorough knowledge of the methods of construction, which inevitably reflect the cultural trends of the time. It is, in fact, these techniques of production and ways of working which provide new aesthetic possibilities. It is the task of the artist and designer to master the expressive potential of the methods and techniques available, and to choose the best solutions to meet man's materials and spiritual needs.

Since such an approach today seems as essential as it is obvious, we tend to underrate the innovative importance it had at the beginning of the twentieth century, when the practice of architecture was still dependent on the dictates of 'Style'. In the same way, taking for granted the use of colour in machines and objects for daily use, we tend to underestimate the gloominess that characterised interiors from the era of the black machine.

Perhaps Mackintosh's most important contribution was his original method of approaching design. It is generally agreed that his planning methods did not make a distinction between interior and exterior and I believe it is right to propose that, for Mackintosh, architecture was an extension of interior design. In short, the object which defines the interior in turn defines the exterior and Mackintosh's overall concept of the exterior. In this, he differs from Frank Lloyd Wright.

We must thus analyse Mackintosh's interiors if we wish to discover the formative principles of his work. For the first time in the history of architecture, we find throughout an entire project a hierarchical organisation of space, a carefully conceived subdivision of levels and a rhythmic distribution of line, form and volume combining to express one unified theme. Such richness of meaning will probably never again be repeated. Mackintosh's precocious flight beyond accepted practice in architecture was somewhat parallel to that of Frank Lloyd Wright. Wright, however, was fortunate in living long enough to establish himself in the 'thirties as one of the leaders of the Modern Movement. Yet Mackintosh's unexecuted design for the Hill House armchair* could be taken for a post-Modern design.

*Roger Billcliffe, *Charles Rennie Mackintosh: The Complete Furniture, Furniture Drawings and Interior Designs*, John Murray, London, third edition, 1986, D1905.21.

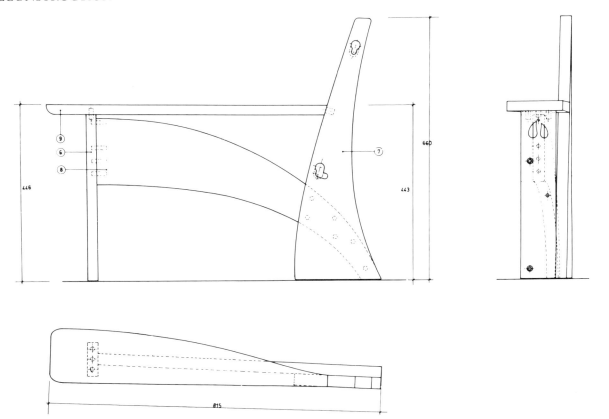

Working drawings for The Hill
House easy chair adapted from a
Mackintosh drawing (Billcliffe
D1905.21).

Production model of The Hill
House easy chair with fabric
based on a Mackintosh textile
design of 1915–23.

Prototype for the easy chair developed from a drawing (Billcliffe D1905.21).

The process of reconstruction begins by considering the furnishing object as a catalyst in space and then examines its expressive and structural elements in the context of contemporary furnishing. An understanding of the reconstruction and use of an object in the modern context is an indispensable aid towards appreciating its rôle in its original environment.

History needs artists like Mackintosh. He shows us how to look for beauty in the free and fluent rhythm of his sequence of simple, linear elements, in his symbolism, and above all in his observation and disciplining of forms as they appear during the various stages of construction. Architectural thought is at present dominated by an unequivocal and unanimous ideological opposition to the Modern Movement, as well as by vehement opposition to all ideas based on a presumed *a priori* conception of architectural forms. Equally controversial in connection with form are the concepts of function and historical identity that for long conditioned the course of design. These theories, which supported the Modern Movement, eventually smothered it, as they proved devoid of imagination and therefore incapable of attaining one of the essential aims of architecture, the expression of an existential experience.

Similarly, interior design, which has suffered from a kind of desperate search through hedonism, autobiography, psychology, symbolism and exoticism, cannot be regarded with anything but suspicion. The mannered and cosmetic approach adopted by designers in an attempt to introduce change, has given rise to 'Design Style' and produced very precarious furniture design.

So architecture is trying to recover its *raison d'être*. The collapse of ideologies that have hitherto influenced our culture has freed our imagination and fostered the rise of originality. Nowadays the task of architecture is above all to recognise and accept all the individual expressions of a people's life and history.

Following the collapse of dogmatic, totalitarian and utilitarian modernistic rules, there has arisen from the depths of consciousness a need for aesthetic satisfaction of a figurative kind. Post-Modern architecture provides for this by freely re-using historical forms with no restriction save practical considerations, and the result is personal, harmonious and congruent. It does not matter whether today's architecture is new or different. What is being done – the re-utilisation of urban centres, the re-establishment of the street for human use, the reconstruction of works by master designers – can be viewed as an architecture of past experiences which brings with it changes in taste and in the understanding of its own history.

151

*C.R. Mackintosh, manuscript of a lecture on *Scotch Baronial Architecture*, 1891, pp33-34, Hunterian Art Gallery, University of Glasgow, Mackintosh Collection.

So strong a demand for aesthetic pleasure can only be answered by an almost subconscious re-interpretation of the particular qualities of form and detail of everyday objects through individual decisions which can be more balanced now that imagination has freed them from the influences of prevailing fashion.

There are at least two ways of approaching the task of reconstruction. One consists of copying the object faithfully, as far as this is actually possible, by recreating every detail with painstaking precision, thus striving to obtain another 'original', yet intending it for modern use. Professor McLaren Young, whose great elegance as a serious and canny scholar I recall with pleasure, used to repeat what Mackintosh had said about the transposition of the past into the present, that it must not be 'strangled in its infancy by undiscriminating, unsympathetic people who will copy . . . ancient examples without beginning to make them conform to modern requirements.'* The undiscriminating and unsympathetic are never in short supply – today as in Mackintosh's time.

The alternative procedure has essential hallmarks: first, the need to retain the original figurative formula which enshrines the designer's stamp, and second, the need for a clear awareness that one must provide for much more than aesthetic satisfaction alone, and go beyond the purely formal realm of figuration in order to meet adequately the new user's needs. These wider values can only be embraced by a mode of thought which takes account of technology and psychology.

When one thinks that reconstruction almost always implies the transposition of the work from the specific system of values of a given culture and time to a different system of values, the number of variables becomes barely manageable and difficult to resolve into a homogenous and functional solution. In fact, what is needed is the mediation of an interpreter who can make the designer's creative itinerary explicit through the technical media selected for the reproduction. Many possibilities emerge from this exercise and from these the mediator must choose the one which in his view the artist himself would have chosen and which would thus realise the artist's intentions.

It is not easy for anyone to recapture a point in an artist's development. It is, however, necessary to do so, for the so-called original art object itself has arisen from continuous mediation by the artist and represents a crystallisation of his interpretative choices. Mackintosh himself made choices in the creation of any piece, and before recapturing it we have thoroughly to explore the tangled paths through the sketches and preliminary designs which led the artist to his ultimate choices, in order to reactivate their aesthetic potential. This is a laborious and difficult procedure in itself even without taking into consideration all the technical possibilities of the materials which have to be used to make objects of unusual form and detailing, or the need to be constantly aware of the risk of imposing the mediator's aesthetic reactions, and to analyse the many other variables which constantly complicate the setting of standards of contemporary objectivity. Without all this effort, what was once excellent may remain confined to the shadows for ever, and ill-considered reconstruction may trivialise an artistically valid work.

Today's re-evaluation of Mackintosh's work, then, should be considered in the context of: 1) changed orientation in taste and the collapse of traditional ideologies; 2) the validity of the artistic creation and the creative procedure; 3) the need for design mediation in furniture reconstruction, making possible the reconstruction and projection of cultural values. Properly carried out, reconstruction reaffirms the past – the continuing values of history – by embracing and endorsing the present with its progress in art, science and technology. Therefore, if Mackintosh's designs are reconstructed with the adjustments required by the present, they will be favourably received by the public because they constitute technically perfect, artistically complete objects available as standard and therefore at reasonable prices.

At this point, it becomes irrelevant whether the reconstructed object is equal to the original. The reconstruction is not intended to encapsulate the past but to realise its hopes. A reconstructed design does not replace the original, but simply explains it.

CHARLES RENNIE MACKINTOSH: A PERSONAL VIEW

Denys Lasdun

In the Glasgow School of Art there is the immediate feeling of a creative mind at work. Charles Rennie Mackintosh clearly did not start, as was so much the custom of his time, from any pre-existing pattern. Mackintosh started from the site and the materials, the existing language of Scottish building and the forms that had obsessed him since he first determined to be an architect. He began with a strong anti-clutter belief for both interior and exterior. He had the true *amor vacui*.

Walls and windows are the basic architectural elements which have been released in Mackintosh's design from the need to form part of conventional and symmetrical patterns, and they speak as things in themselves which can take part in the archetypal play of solid and void and thus become architectural elements of really quite unexpected weight and eloquence.

It is not so much that Mackintosh invented new forms as that he used existing forms in ways that he found appropriate to the existing situation – the glorification in fact of the thing itself – one of the greatest avenues of success for British architects through the ages.

In the north façade of the School of Art, between the big windows, the design goes beyond function – fusing both into architecture and into art – skilful, daring, imaginative, austere.

In the library, there is an extraordinary air of frozen excitement. The lines are dynamic and everywhere the stress is on the manipulation and control of space. The structural form is revealed and emphasised; the timber itself speaks. Posts, brackets, rafters organised within recognisable modules of measurement speak of timeless space, of a place of assembly which would be appropriate to any age. It reminds me of the brooding mystery of a Japanese temple.

It is a building that we should cherish intently. It so clearly exemplifies all that is best in the revolt against historicism and clutter. It is still a powerful modern building, a powerful Scottish building and one that proclaims something of the universal essence of architecture.

Windyhill creates in its situation a grave and serious presence with large expanses of wall and an articulation of small windows like the typical Scottish stone house of the seventeenth century. The Hill House maintains a similar gravity – nothing has ever got so far away from the Baroque as the Scottish vernacular – but it is a presence of the twentieth century. Again the architecture is a synthesis of distinct elements arising from their placing and their relation to each other. Mackintosh knew that a house near Glasgow was not the place for wide expanses of glass as in the north façade of the Glasgow School of Art, and he had the positive feeling that a home should be enclosed and sheltered and secure. Without a range of small windows he would also have lost one vital element in the eloquent organisation of façades, and he could not have produced the play of solid and void which he took to be the essence of Scottish vernacular.

Again the functional features such as the chimney breast are used as architectural elements; the entrance combines with the chimney breast to create a major stress on the same lines as that in the centre of the north façade of the Glasgow School of Art. The staircase is splendidly integrated into the north façade at The Hill House and the juxtaposition of the various elements on that side shows with what assurance Mackintosh developed the somewhat thin and frosty air of Scottish vernacular and transformed it into a living style of the early twentieth century – highly characteristic of the period but without in any way compromising its profound originality and individuality.

The Hill House and the Glasgow School of Art stand out as the two undoubted masterpieces of Mackintosh.

While he was the progenitor of the most creative side of modern architecture – of all that which, in the confusion of this brutal century, has tried to uphold the central truths of architecture, without compromising in any way with historicism or eclecticism – Mackintosh nevertheless remained throughout his career a Scottish, if not a Glaswegian, architect. He felt the Scottish vernacular was a national style that was due for transfiguration in modern terms – Scottish, modern and alive.

Has any other architect ever been as free from prejudices and presuppositions?

EPILOGUE

Patrick Nuttgens

The papers delivered at the 1983 conference and published in this book are about both the influence of Charles Rennie Mackintosh upon the scene at his time and the influence of that scene upon Charles Rennie Mackintosh. The conference was, in essence, about the turn of the century, and its constantly hovering message concerned the relevance of Mackintosh and his contemporaries to the architecture of our own day, unsettled and various but possibly finding a new certainty as it rediscovers the richness and quality of an earlier period.

The start of that architectural period was the search for a free style, influenced but not confined by history. In the work of all the major figures the same fundamental characteristics can be found – the use of nature and natural form as a key to the new style, the use of a geometry in which typical forms are the whiplash curve, the parabola and various three-dimensional shapes, inspiration through drawing and painting (of which all the major architects were outstanding practitioners), the rediscovery of the vernacular and vernacular colour, the need to appeal to all the senses including touch, and the influence as never before of architectural publications and magazines on a popular scale.

From those common characteristics, it is possible to extract a number of central themes and questions. Fundamental and frequently recurring was the question of style. In a sense the movement was anti-style and its leaders were anxious to escape from the historical precedents. But that meant that they were constantly retreating into styles or at the least into an obsession with the 'idea' of style. Architects questioned about style, said E. W. Godwin, should answer, 'It is my own.'

Second, the architects of the period were obsessed with the problem of originality. The most obviously original buildings might be in zoos, as the needs of animals and not just the needs of the visitors were taken into account, but a more profound originality was to be found in the planning of familiar buildings, in houses and churches and schools and colleges. The freedom made possible by structural discoveries inspired architects (none more than Mackintosh himself) to play with space and make plans that exploit that freedom and delight in space for its own sake.

Third, and in contrast with what happened later, they produced an architecture with individuality. It was an individuality not so much of general massing (as can be seen in many buildings of the period) as of particular solutions to detailed problems of structure and form that could be developed to lead to a general theory. There never was a better time for door handles and window fasteners and cupboards and fireplaces and baths and basins.

Fourth, the work of most of the architects reveals the importance they attached to training in manual skills. The influence upon building of the technology of the Industrial Revolution must, in the long run, have been profound, but it may not have had as much effect upon the architecture of the turn of the century – or perhaps the speakers at the conference avoided its complications.

Fifth, what everyone was clear about was the importance of colour – probably colour intrinsic to materials rather than applied colour. Again, this was a characteristic lost in the architecture of the International Style of the next generation.

The architecture of the period revealed, in short, a remarkable unity of function, structure and form. It delighted in the play of light and space. This was what its pioneers set out to achieve – a genuinely free (and thus modern) architecture.

It seemed to me that this conference, with all its richness and variety of subject matter, left a number of questions (or challenges) open at the end. One concerned education and training given to architects. The skills they need are particular skills rather than the generalised ones that have tended to be taught in recent years; a genuine originality is more likely to be found in solving particular problems, as the architects who were discussed during the conference had manifestly discovered. In pursuit of this end, there could be no escape from the need to be able to draw, for drawing is more than a way of communicating: it is also a way to understand what is happening in an existing building and what should happen in a new one.

The next challenge concerned the vernacular. For, as the architects of the turn of the century discovered for themselves and as architectural historians have been confirming ever since, vernacular architecture – the unsophisticated houses of everyman, built with traditional skills but without aesthetic choosiness – is genuinely an international phenomenon, worldwide and varied. It was one of the great discoveries of the period that ordinary people's buildings provided an inexhaustibly rich vocabulary for a new architecture. The implications have not yet been fully explored.

Finally, the phrase 'National and International' in the title of the conference on which this book is based is more meaningful than it might at first have appeared. The relationship between the national and the international was crucial to any understanding of the situation at the turn of the century – as it is again now. The truly national style is found not by looking inwards at one's own scene but by looking outwards. A preoccupation with the immediate surroundings and an exaggerated idea of their importance leads to provincialism – a danger well-known in Scotland. True nationalism consists in looking out at the world but seeing it differently from the way other people see it because of where you are looking from. The world is different because of where you are.

The influence of Scotland in general and of Mackintosh in particular was thus international. However much he might be criticised, however unsuccessful he might seem to have been, the personality of Mackintosh kept coming through – in designs, in artefacts, in buildings, in an all-pervasive attitude that had little to do with theory (Mackintosh produced no theory worthy of the name) but everything to do with practice and with products. In his limping, unsatisfactory way, he dominated the European scene. As Olbrich, no mean designer himself, wrote wearily one day, 'Dear Mackintosh, You are the worthy one'.

INDEX

This index is restricted to proper names and covers the main text and the picture captions but not the footnotes. Page numbers of picture captions are given in italics.

Buildings and institutions are grouped under town, city or state (e.g. most Mackintosh buildings are listed under Glasgow). Churches are always listed under their town or city. Where a geographical reference would include only a single building, this is given instead under its own name (e.g. Maison Coilliot, Lille). Where it has seemed useful to provide them, cross-references have been given from architects to the main locations under which their buildings are listed.

PICTURE CREDITS

Illustrations are reproduced by courtesy of the following:

Annan Gallery, Glasgow 112b

John H.G. Archer 58, 64, 65, 66, 67, 68

Cassina 150a, 150b, 151

Greene and Greene Library 90a, 90b, 91, 92b, 94a, 96a

Historisches Museum der Stadt Wien 99b, 100b

Neil Holland 21, 23

Thomas Howarth 40a, 40b, 40c, 40d, 49b, 50, 51a, 51b, 52a, 52b, 54

Hunterian Art Gallery, University of Glasgow, Mackintosh Collection 48, 100a

Don Kalec 76, 78, 79a, 79b, 80a, 80b, 82, 83, 84a, 84b, 85a, 85b, 86, 87a, 87b, 88a, 88b, 89a, 89b

Randell L. Makinson 95

Mitchell Library, Glasgow 99a

Österreichisches Museum für angewandte Kunst 115a, 115b, 115c, 117a, 117b, 118, 119

Polytechnic University of Barcelona, Cátedra Gaudí 141, 142, 144, 145, 148

Perth Museum and Art Gallery 36c

Marvin Rand 2, 93, 94b, 94c, 96b, 97a, 97b

Royal Commission on the Ancient and Historical Monuments of Scotland 33a, 33b, 34a, 36a, 36b, 36c, 38

Scottish Development Department, Historic Buildings and Monuments 34a, 35

Sellers Collection 70

W.J. Smith 9

Victoria & Albert Museum 24